Beyond
Book Indexing

EDITED BY DIANE BRENNER
AND MARILYN ROWLAND

Beyond Book Indexing

EDITED BY DIANE BRENNER
AND MARILYN ROWLAND

AMERICAN
SOCIETY OF
INDEXERS

ISBN 1-57387-081-1

Published by
Information Today, Inc.
143 Old Marlton Pike
Medford, NJ 08055

in association with

The American Society of Indexers, Inc.
PO Box 39366
Phoenix, AZ 85069-9366

Printed in the United States of America

Managing Editor: Janet M. Spavlik
Book Designers: Patricia F. Kirkbride
Jeremy M. Pellegrin
Indexer: Janet Perlman
Editors: Diane Brenner
Marilyn Rowland

Table of Contents

Preface

In 1998, Marilyn Rowland approached me with a proposal for this book. The idea was exciting then, and its relevance has only increased in the past year. Marilyn and Diane Brenner have done an excellent job in bringing it all together so quickly. The concepts and discussion are "fresh," and the contributors give voice to many provocative ideas. Their practical experiences, as detailed here, provide the "nuts and bolts" of how they have created non-traditional electronic indexes. They also give advice about Web sites and home pages and the uses of email discussion lists. It is a full tour of the "new world" facing indexers—how our skills create new opportunities and how we should pursue those opportunities. I am excited by our role in this lively, evolving world.

On behalf of the American Society of Indexers (ASI), I would like to thank all the authors: Jan Wright, Lynn Moncrief, Dwight Walker, Kevin Broccoli and Gerry Van Ravenswaay, Seth Maislin, Marilyn Rowland, Susan Holbert, X Bonnie Woods, Rachel Rice, and Dan Connolly. Diane Brenner served as co-editor, and Janet Perlman created the index.

We are also grateful for the assistance of Information Today, Inc.'s staff—in particular, John Bryans, Dorothy Pike, Janet Spavlik and Heather Rudolph. This is the seventh book we have done with them, and we appreciate their continued commitment to producing educational material related to indexing.

For additional information about ASI, contact:

American Society of Indexers
P.O. Box 39366
Phoenix, AZ 85069-9366
Voice: (602) 979-5514
Fax: (602) 530-4088
Email: info@asindexing.org
Internet: http://www.asindexing.org

For a list of ASI publications, sign onto the Internet address above or contact Information Today, Inc., ASI's official publisher. To order ASI books and pamphlets contact:

Information Today, Inc.
143 Old Marlton Pike
Medford, NJ 08055
Phone: 1-800-300-9868 (or 609-654-6266)
Fax: (609) 654-4309
Email: custserv@infotoday.com

Enid L. Zafran
Publications Committee Chair

Introduction

Are you curious about new indexing technologies? Are you interested in developing Web site indexes or creating innovative ways of accessing online resources, multimedia projects, or online help? Do you want to develop new skills and marketing possibilities? Welcome to *Beyond Book Indexing*.

Most of us are at least semi-computer literate. We use dedicated indexing software to create our indexes, and we know how to go online. Our email use is not just personal but also for professional communication; and we participate in online professional discussion groups such as INDEX-L. But many of us remain inveterate back-of-the-book indexers.

Today there are numerous indexing possibilities, including a plethora of computer-related information-handling and presentation needs just waiting for the enterprising indexer. In this volume, a group of experienced and talented indexers acquaint you with some of the possibilities now available in computer-based, CD-ROM, and Web-related indexing.

We start with Section 1, Jan Wright's introduction to "The World of Embedded Indexing." Embedded indexing has become an increasingly popular technique (at least among publishers) for producing back-of-the-book indexes. Currently, its most common print application is in the creation of computer books, documentation, and manuals. Lynn Moncrief's article "Indexing Computer-Related Documents" provides in-depth information on how to put together indexes for this type of material, using both embedded and traditional indexing techniques. The embedding skills discussed in these two chapters resemble those needed to develop the indexes discussed in the remainder of the book.

In Section 2, the focus turns to "Web Indexing," a term that is not yet well-defined and ranges from creating directories of Web sites on specific topics, to indexing individual sites and online publications, to creating whole new navigation structures that provide users with clear and easy access to Web site contents. This section presents a very exciting, though inchoate realm, where traditional book structures no longer exist, and where the information industry is experiencing a growing need to develop creative and effective access and navigation approaches (i.e., indexes). In this volume, we are pleased to include contributions from five skilled and adventurous pioneers who have explored both the theoretical and practical aspects of Web site indexing.

Dwight Walker in "Subject-Oriented Web Indexing" opens with a discussion on how to create Web indexes that can serve as directories to other Web sites. He shares experience gleaned from developing and running a Web indexing course out of his home base in Australia. Kevin Broccoli and Gerry Van Ravenswaay in "Anchors Away!," give an overview of the exciting and as yet uncharted world of indexing Web sites. Seth Maislin in "Ripping Out the Pages" delves into Web index design and structure, providing numerous concrete examples of effective Web indexes. Finally, Marilyn Rowland in "Plunging In: Creating a Web Site Index for an Online Newsletter" details her experience working on her prize-winning index for Acxiom Corporation's online newsletter, *Case-in-Point*.

In Section 3, we turn to "Special Topics in Computer-based Indexing." Marilyn Rowland's article "<META> Tags" explains what these tags are, why they are important, and how to include them in our Web sites and indexes. Susan Holbert follows with "How To Index Windows-Based Online Help." Her overview of this important specialized area provides insights and practical suggestions for both indexers and technical writers. Finally, X Bonnie Woods in "Envisioning the Word: Multimedia CD-ROM Indexing" introduces us to the fluid and challenging world of multimedia CD-ROM indexing. She shares her experience as part of the team responsible for creating and implementing the "index" for a huge CD-ROM project, Microsoft's *Encarta Africana*.

In the final section, we provide several articles to help you use online resources to expand your marketing and employment opportunities. Marilyn Rowland's third article, "Web Site Design for Indexers," should inspire all procrastinators to get moving and create their own Web sites. Rachel Rice details the process of "Putting Sample Indexes on Your Web Site." She provides a template that will make HTML coding easier. Finally, Dan Connolly in "The Many Uses of Email Discussion Lists" presents an overview of an important resource that can provide freelancers with professional information, support, and marketing opportunities.

Most of the articles include references and online resources to point you to tools and information you'll need to pursue these subjects in greater depth. At the end of the book we have compiled a glossary that explains terms that you might be unfamiliar with.

Once you've read these articles, you may feel you need to learn HTML or Web design. You may want to invest in new software or hardware to upgrade your system. You may decide to present and sell yourself differently. By embracing these opportunities, you will gain new skills, new employment options, and new marketing strategies. You will also feel the exhilaration of being on the leading edge of indexing technology. Wishing you all exciting indexing adventures.

Diane Brenner
Worthington, MA

Marilyn Rowland
Falmouth, MA

Contributors

Diane Brenner

dbrenner@javanet.com

http://www.dianebrenner.com

Diane Brenner has been a freelance indexer and copyeditor for ten years. During the past year, she has become heavily involved with embedded indexing and the indexing of computer manuals. She considers herself a generalist, a fact reinforced by her eclectic education (art history, MSW, and doctorate in environmental toxicology/ statistics), as well as by her broad range of interests. She works from her office in Worthington, Massachusetts. This is her second collaboration with Marilyn Rowland, the first an article on "Indexing Art and Art History Books" for the ASI publication, *Indexing Specialties: History*. She has recently become a member of the ASI Web Committee.

Kevin Broccoli

Broccoli Information Management

brocindx@in4web.com

http://www.bim.net

Kevin Broccoli is a freelancer indexer and information architect who creates indexes for print publications, online help, and Web sites. He is Vice President/Program Chair for the New York Chapter of ASI, Coordinator of ASI's Special Interest Groups, and co-coordinator of ASI's Web Indexing SIG. He has written articles for online magazines on Web indexing and is a pioneer in the usage of indexes for Web sites and intranets.

Daniel A. Connolly

Word For Word Indexing Services

connolly@neca.com

http://www.WFWIndex.necaweb.com

Dan Connolly operates Word For Word Indexing Services in Woodstock, Connecticut. He is a member of ASI and the Massachusetts Society of Indexers. Dan has completed the Basic Indexing course of the USDA Graduate School, and has founded and manages Indexstudents, an email discussion list concerned with indexer education and professional development (http://www.onelist.com/subscribe.cgi/indexstudents). Dan focuses primarily on indexing educational and psychological texts.

Susan Holbert

Indexing Services
susanh@world.std.com
http://www.abbington.com/holbert
Since 1980 Susan Holbert has indexed hundreds of books and manuals for publishing, business, technology, and government clients, ranging from medical, financial, and engineering software to the autobiography of First Lady Rosalynn Carter. As a technical manuals specialist, she has developed techniques that go beyond traditional indexing practices to meet the specific needs of documentation users. She has created two popular indexing seminars, *Basic Indexing Skills* and *How to Index User Manuals and Online Help*, available as training workshops or on video. She has given numerous public presentations. Her articles have appeared in both local and national publications. She authored the indexing sections of the Lotus *Style Guide* and the Addison Wesley Longman *Authors' Guide*. She also designed and markets wINDEX, an indexing software program.

Seth Maislin

Focus Information Services
smaislin@world.std.com
Seth Maislin indexed more than 70 books in 1998 and supervised the indexing of several others. Focus Information Services, his Massachusetts-based company, has participated in several intriguing contracts, including the indexing of America Online and the cataloging of more than 250,000 clip art images. Seth is also the in-house indexer at O'Reilly & Associates, an internationally renowned publisher of computer books and software. He provides consulting services in indexing and information architecture to both public and private audiences and is an experienced speaker. Currently Seth serves on the ASI Board of Directors, chairs its W3C Committee, and serves as liaison to the ASI Web Committee and as Chair of Continuing Studies for the Massachusetts Chapter. He is also webmaster for the Indexing SIG of the Society for Technical Communication (STC).

Lynn Moncrief

techndex@PACBELL.NET
Lynn Moncrief was an Electronics Technician in the U.S. Navy before becoming a technical writer. After a few years of technical writing, she founded TECHindex & Docs and became an indexer. She has recently retired from indexing and devotes most of her time to artwork.

Rachel Rice

Directions Unlimited
racric@together.net
http://homepages.together.net/~racric

Rachel Rice is a part-time indexer and full-time psychiatric crisis intervention clinician who spends too much time on the Internet. Her indexing interests are varied and include psychology, animals, Judaica, business, self-help, and how-to books.

Marilyn J. Rowland

Marisol Productions
marisol@marisol.com
http://www.marisol.com

Marilyn Rowland has indexed books and periodicals for over 30 years, full-time for the last 12 years or so, and in and around other careers as an urban and environmental planner and energy conservation manager. She has a masters degree in city and regional planning. She enjoys the challenge and diversity of embedded indexes, Web indexes, Web site design, and new ways of making information available to people. Marilyn is chair of the ASI Web Site Committee and serves as co-webmaster for the ASI site (http://www.asindexing.org). She created and maintains the Massachusetts Society of Indexers Web site (http://www.marisol.com/maasi/). She also writes on a wide range of topics and produces and directs local cable access television programs.

Gerry Van Ravenswaay

GVR Information Services, Ltd.
gvrindex@xsite.net
http://www.xsite.net/~gvrindex

Gerry Van Ravenswaay, of Chicago, Illinois, has been an ASI member for nine years and a full-time, freelance indexer for four years. He is chair of the Chicago/Great Lakes Chapter, co-coordinator of ASI's Web Indexing SIG, member of ASI's Web Committee, and co-author of the Society's online index. He has also written indexes for the Chicago/Great Lakes Chapter's Web site and his own Web site. His interest in indexing for online documents was sparked by freelancing for *Encyclopaedia Britannica's* Internet Guide (BIG), the forerunner of eBlast.

Dwight Walker

WWWalker Web Development
wwwalker@kagi.com
http://www.wwwalker.com.au/

Dwight Walker is a director of WWWalker Web Development, a computer consultancy based in Sydney, Australia. He has a Bachelor of Science in computer science and a Graduate Diploma in Information Management and Librarianship. He has worked as a programmer, systems programmer, and technical support person before moving into research, publishing, librarianship, technical writing, and Web development. He has been active in the Australian Society of Indexers' NSW and National Committees for several years. In 1994 he started out as the first Webmaster of the

Australian Society of Indexers where he pioneered the science of Web indexing. In addition, he is editor of the *AusSI Newsletter*, has spoken at AusSI conferences on Web indexing, and started the AusSI Web indexing prize, of which he is still coordinator. He was appointed the first Australian Pacific corresponding editor of *The Indexer*, an international journal based in the UK. In his business he regularly writes an Internet column for *Online Currents*, an Australian online database journal for librarians. With WWWalker he set up and led online Web indexing courses for many Americans in 1998 over the Internet and led a Web indexing seminar at the 1998 ASI Seattle conference. From this initiative, ASI has began its Web Indexing SIG. Based on the Web indexing course, he publishes *Introduction to Web Indexing* on the WWWalker Web site and is busy designing WEBIX, a Web indexing program for Webmasters and indexers to better organize Web sites or link databases.

X Bonnie Woods

xbonnie@xwoods.com
X Bonnie Woods is a painter who likes words and who delights in a challenging editorial project. She was the Executive Director of Product Completion and an editor for *Encarta Africana*, a multimedia CD-ROM produced by Microsoft. Currently she is Executive Editor and Senior Analyst at Dynamic Diagrams, a division of Cadmus Journal Services, designing information architecture for large online publications. She is a member of the College Art Association and the Massachusetts Society of Indexers as well as ASI.

Jan C. Wright

Wright Information Indexing Services
ANCW@wrightinformation.com
http://www.wrightinformation.com
Jan C. Wright is the owner of Wright Information Indexing Services, which has provided print and online indexing to companies such as Microsoft, Asymetrix, Visio, PeachPit Press, and Sakson and Taylor. She has served as a judge for the Society for Technical Communication's (STC) annual publications competition, has a Master's Degree in Library Science, and uses her many years of experience as a professional librarian to help make her indexes more user-friendly. She is an ASI member and serves as co-editor of *A to Z: The Newsletter of STC's Indexing SIG*.

Part 1
Beyond Stand-Alone Indexes: Embedded Indexing

Chapter 1

The World of Embedded Indexing

Jan C. Wright © 1999

Here's the scenario: Your favorite client calls to tell you they are changing their processes. "We've decided to go completely electronic and embed the indexing in the files. Can you do that?" It looks like your life and the way you do your work is going to change if you say yes. But before you do, make sure you know enough about the new process to know whether you want to take on the project. Embedded indexing brings a whole new level of complexity to the indexing process. You will need to incorporate new software technologies and special editing/index-compiling skills with the traditional thought and analysis that has always gone into the indexing process.

What do we mean when we say you can embed indexing into files? The simplest answer is the one that Nancy Mulvany gives in *Indexing Books*:

Embedded indexing software is generally a feature found in word processing or page design software such as WordPerfect or Ventura Publisher. Embedded indexing software allows the indexer to insert index entries (or tags for entries) directly into the document's text files.

In other words, instead of writing an index in CINDEX, Macrex, or SkyIndex, you put the index entries directly into the same files that are used to create the book. Many companies use Microsoft Word, PageMaker, FrameMaker, or Quark to create their manuals and books, editing, layout, and printing directly from the program files. Pasting up pages manually and creating galleys are not part of electronic publishing. Everything lives in files, from the time it is written until the time it goes to the publisher's printing plates.

When you embed indexing codes into these files, the publisher has no worry about what page numbers go into the index until the very end. If needed, files can go through layout, content and copy-edit changes even after indexing is completed. This approach also permits indexing and text to be re-used in the next edition or even converted into hyperactive links!

HOW EMBEDDING WORKS

Whether you use PageMaker or Quark, Word or WordPerfect, there are some universal features of embedded indexing. Instead of preset pages, DTP (desktop publishing) products are fluid. The text "floats" on the page in rivers, and moves around as the layout artists arrange pictures and other design elements. This means that the location of the subject you are indexing can float around as well.

For example, let's say you are indexing a section that discusses rubber bands, and right now, it is on page 4.

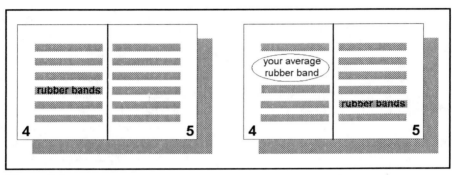

Figure 1.1

Suppose an artist then inserts a picture of a rubber band above the paragraph where rubber bands are first discussed. That picture could displace enough text to push your sentence over onto page 5. In electronic publishing, this type of text movement is very common. As a result, pages are usually not finalized until very close to the end of the publishing process. This is called "setting the page breaks" or "breaking the pages," and until the process is completed (i.e., "frozen") the text can move around, or float. From the perspective of traditional indexing, this is a nightmare.

With embedded indexing, you insert ("embed") main entries and subentries directly into the text as sections of code that move along with the text. These codes are then "compiled" by the indexing software to produce a more or less finished index with the correct page numbers inserted for each coded locator. The codes are usually hidden (not visible) when the book is printed. In the first example, let's say you have inserted some indexing code to mark the discussion of rubber bands. If you were to compile the index, the indexing software would assign page 4 as the page number for that entry. After the picture is inserted, and the text has flowed to the next page, a newly compiled index would show page 5 as the locator for that entry.

Adding pictures can change the location of text, as can adding text or rearranging paragraphs. Enlarging the text size, reducing it, or changing the heading format can alter text placement. Through all these changes, the coded (embedded) index entries float along attached to their paragraphs or lines of text. It does not matter what page they are on, when the index is compiled (that is, generated by the embedded indexing software), the page number that is attached to the index entry will correspond to the place where the text ends up. The index entries survive all these changes, allowing the publisher freedom to rearrange the book or update it without worrying about the "right" page numbers until the very end.

Publishers are interested in having the index entries embedded as part of a book's files for many reasons:

- Indexing can begin before the page proofs are finalized. This means a quicker "time to publication." For some publishers this is the primary reason for embedding. Chapters can be sent for indexing as they are completed, not necessarily in the order they appear in the book.

- Revisions prior to publication, or new editions with changes in layout and relatively minor text adjustments, will not require re-indexing. A relatively quick review of the existing indexing may suffice. Since the index is not tied to page numbers, changing the location of page breaks does not matter. You simply recompile the index and it reflects these changes.

- Indexing that lives in the files can be used in other formats. They can, for example, be converted into an online interactive index that allows readers to jump to the right page.

- Translators need only translate the index entries, not worry about updating the page numbers as well.

FILES, FILES, FILES

If you plan to do embedded indexing, you must become an expert in file management. A book built using DTP software lives in files and you must find a way to keep track of which ones you have, which files you have completed, and which are the new versions. You may receive one giant file, 25 small files, or anything in between, depending on how the production people work and which software was used.

One concept that is absolutely critical to understand is that of "live files." Here's a possible scenario: You receive ten files for embedding by email from the client. As you start working on the files and entering indexing codes, your client decides to do last minute copyediting and changes some of the art work. When you email back your set of files, your client now has two sets, and they are different! One set has her copyedits, the other set has your index entries, and there is no way to merge them!

As the indexer, you have to be very clear about who has the editing rights to the one set of files that is "live." Think of it as the old game of the "hot potato." If you have the set of "live" files, your client must know that you have them and agree not to make any changes until you return the files; otherwise you will end up with major problems. Always ask if you are the only person currently making changes to the files.

THE EMBEDDING PROCESS

The embedding process is different from traditional indexing. You will need to make sure your client understands the steps in the indexing process as well, because you will be trying to work out a good time for you to have these files solely in your hands. Here is an overview.

- Copy the file. As soon as you receive them, make backup copies of all files. This is a critical step! You always want to retain a clean copy of the original file.

- Read the text. This step is the same for all indexing projects, embedded or not: Read the material for audience, content, approach, scope, etc.

- Create entries. This part can happen in stages. Ideally, of course, indexing should start at the beginning of the book and end at the end, though with electronic publishing, this does not always happen. You can exchange files back and forth as needed with the client during this stage, as you can only work on one file at a time. Each DTP software package handles the process of creating coded entries differently, and you should run some tests to make sure you are handling items like cross references and special sorting correctly.

- Compile the index for editing. To edit the index you will need to compile it into its formatted version. Most DTP packages, unlike dedicated indexing software, do not display the index while you are building it, so you must compile it to see how it looks. You will need to have all the files solely at your disposal for this step. Print out the compiled index to look at, edit, and work from.

- Edit and incorporate edits. Once compiled, the index is edited for consistency and scope. This task, which is so simple in stand-alone indexing, is much more difficult in embedded indexing because most embedded indexes are only snapshots of the codes as they exist at this point in time. You cannot make changes in the compiled index itself, you must go back to the original file, find the page and entry, and then make your changes in the code itself. If you do not edit errors in the code, the next time you compile the index, all your errors will reappear.

If the index is not going to be reused, and the publisher is interested in embedding simply as a time-saving tool (for them), then they may allow the indexer the luxury of editing the final compiled index in a stand-alone index.

If the index is to be used again, or for other purposes such as transfer into HTML format, the editing process is much more complex. Often, clients do not understand this step, and think you can do it one chapter at a time. Make sure they understand that you have to change the erroneous code *each* and *every* time it occurs. Since the code for that particular heading or subheading may occur in different chapters throughout the book, you need access to *all* the files so you can edit code wherever it appears. For example, you may have a reference to "cameras" and discover it needs to be changed to "photographic supplies." Codes for these entries may currently be in chapters 2, 7, and 8. You would have to go back to each chapter and, by hand, change each coded entry.

First edit on the printout, as incorporating the edits is a tedious task. Work through the printout making notes on what to change, then go back to the files and make the changes in the original codes.

- **Recompile the edited index.** Check that you did your edits correctly.
- **Proof the index.** This stage is the same as in traditional indexing.
- **Handoff.** Transmit the finished index and all files to the client.

PROCESS ISSUES

If you decide to try embedded indexing, you will need to become familiar with each software package's unique embedding techniques. Writing an index using embedded codes is both easier and harder than writing in stand-alone software. On the plus side, automatic page numbering means you do not have to worry about getting every page number right and makes updating the index after layout changes very easy.

Most DTP software packages are closed systems; i.e., it is difficult to interchange files developed using different software packages, and the electronic publishing process is basically a closed process. The indexer usually must work in the same files that the production people need to be tweaking for final edits and printing. This creates a time strain that usually does not happen in stand-alone indexing.

You will need to make sure that your computer matches the configuration of the production machines your client is using. The software version should be the same; special macros, templates, or add-ons that affect layout should be installed; and, most critically, the printer drivers and the font setup should match. Otherwise, font substitution could make the pages change enough to throw off indexing. Just think what would happen if this page's font, for instance, turned into Courier 14 point text. It can throw off captions, tables, and line breaks enough for you not to know how the piece will look when printed. And yes, even though text floats and page breaks change, a complex page layout can become unreadable if your fonts differ.

Make sure you get a printed copy of the piece before indexing so you can see the page layout. You may be unable to read the piece and index it entirely on screen. Most embedding software packages hog the screen when displaying the index modules, and it is hard to figure out where on the page you are and where the page ranges should end. Depending on which product you are using, the text may float down simply because you have put in index codes, even though they do not display in the final printed piece.

Creating page ranges is one of the major weaknesses of embedded indexing. In traditional indexing, you only include page ranges if the text continues for more than one page. In embedded indexing, you need to worry about what will happen if the text floats to another page, even though it all seems to be contained on one page now. You must decide to use either a single page number or a range. When a topic starts near the bottom of an existing page, you need to consider "What is the likelihood that in the final edition, this will break across these pages? Should I use a page range here?" In some ways, you are trying to second-guess the final look of the book before it is done.

Many indexers limit the number of page ranges because of this guesswork. Some indexers only use ranges for topics that cover more than a page and a half, so they are sure there is truly need for a range. Others add identical code to both the beginning and end of paragraphs to ensure that the ranges will be caught if they occur.

An embedded index takes longer to create than a stand-alone index. Creating page ranges is a complex process, and at times requires counting or highlighting paragraphs or duplicating code entries. Each software package places its own demands on your computer's memory, so use a fast machine. Your usual average pages-indexed-per-day goals will probably be difficult to reach, especially when you are indexing a complex piece. Editing will still require a third of the total time and may take even more if you have to go back to the original text and edit multiple coded entries. Be sure to allow yourself enough time.

Also, if you need to correct code throughout the document, make sure you can have access to all the files for long time periods. If you have to wait for files, you waste time. During the editing process, nearly every entry gets changed somewhat, and since editing happens in alphabetical order, that means edits happen in haphazard order. Your clients may not understand this and may not want to give you all the files at once, so you must educate them about this portion of the process.

If anyone works with the files after you have finished indexing, make sure they know not to delete the index tags. Your client needs to establish processes for moving the tags when paragraphs move during rewriting and for handling deleted text. Text added in the middle of an already-coded discussion can throw off the page ranges and should be checked carefully for its impact on the index. You are the only person who understands what can happen to the index, so you should have an opportunity to review it.

Many of the embedded indexing programs do not handle small caps or the italicized text you may need in your entries. Adding a series of asterisks (***) to the end of problem entries will allow you to search for entries that have special requirements in the compiled index text file that is created at the very end of the indexing process.

Also, make sure you know how clients want to format cross-references. Publishers differ greatly with respect to the formatting of *see* and *see also* references. You might need to employ certain tricks, such as entering "zsee also" instead of "see also" to your coded entries to make sure they appear appropriately at the bottom of subheading lists. The "z" can be removed easily in the final index text without returning to the original codes.

At the end of the process, the index is compiled and placed into the publication. Remind your client that this index is a snapshot. If they move or change text in the files, the index is not automatically updated. They must recompile to make those changes appear in the index file.

EMBEDDING A STAND-ALONE INDEX INTO FILES AFTER EDITING

Embedding a stand-alone index can eliminate some of the difficulties associated with the embedding process. Essentially you build the index traditionally in a dedicated indexing program, the way indexers usually work. After the editing phase, you re-sort the index into page number order and then return to the client's files and enter the entries as codes at the appropriate places in the publication files.

Why would you want to do this? Because this is one way to keep the files free for the production staff to make changes up to the last minute. If the production staff cannot afford the time to send live files to the indexer, but still want embedded entries, this could be a viable choice for you and for them.

An advantage of this method is that if the publisher can break the pages and paginate them, they can go to press with the stand-alone index file and embed the codes after the book goes to press. This is often a great idea if the book is to be translated or converted to an online format. You get the best of both worlds—speed and codes.

According to Ed Malick of Frame Technology Corporation, this technique is used for building Frame's manual indexes. Frame added the capacity to create stand-alone indexes into FrameMaker because it allows indexers to develop indexes using the tools that work best for indexing, and eliminates final pagination changes. The time used for embedding a stand-alone index is less than it would be to write the entire index within FrameMaker itself.

To adapt this technique to most DTP software packages is easy: the indexer can start with printouts and write the index in stand-alone format. If you are going to embed the index *before* going to press, instead of using page numbers, consider numbering each paragraph and using those numbers instead. This simplifies finding the exact spot for codes later on. If you are going to press with the stand-alone file and then embedding *later*, the publisher must establish firm page breaks and minimize changes to the files, and you must use the page numbers.

After the index is edited, generate a file that shows each entry sorted by number rather than alphabetically. Then, open the production files, start the embedding and work your way through the list. Generate an index periodically and check it against the original verify the work. Or if you want, wait until the piece goes to press and then embed the codes.

GETTING STARTED IN EMBEDDED INDEXING

So which software package should you learn, or, more importantly, buy to get started in embedded indexing? You may already have your first package on your machine. Take a look to see if you have Microsoft Word or another word processor with an indexing module in it. Word processors are used heavily in the publishing of technical books, not just for writing, but for sending pieces to press. You can learn how to use the indexing modules from the online help and experiment with the indexing modules until you feel comfortable and indexing becomes predictable. You can also develop some speed-enhancing tricks such as using the copy/paste feature to facilitate entry of similar headings or by creating auto-text "macros" for frequently used terms or complex acronyms.

Should you buy a DTP package so that you can offer services to more clients? This is a difficult question because these packages are very expensive. A commitment to PageMaker or FrameMaker costs $500 or more, and most clients will not purchase these packages for you. Each update also costs money, and different clients frequently use different or older versions. Can you afford to keep PageMaker 5.0 for one client, and 6.5 for another? Do you want to shell out more money to update your version because your client has? It is an expensive market to be dabbling with when you are first starting out.

These packages also require a hefty computer. You are working with large files that require quite a bit of processing power. Some of your clients may produce intensive four-color pieces that can require a lot of memory just to open the files. And your indexing process usually runs across all of the files, demanding a lot of processing power for compiling. You should be running the same operating system as your clients, using the same installed fonts and the same printer drivers. This requires an investment in your time to make sure all these factors are working together correctly. And don't forget the fun part of sending or returning files over the Internet, a process that can run into problems as well.

One way to experiment with the more expensive packages would be to take a course at a local community college computer lab. Introductory PageMaker and FrameMaker classes are taught nationwide, and lab time could be used to figure out how the indexing works and whether you want to proceed with learning (and buying) the tool. This is an inexpensive way to get a taste, and as a side benefit, you will learn layout, which will help you understand your clients' work.

I would recommend first learning the least expensive package—your word-processing package—and see if advertising this expertise gets you additional clients. Then, if a project comes along requiring one of the more expensive packages, take the plunge, but only if you are sure that you'll be paid.

WORKING WITH CLIENTS

As you can see, embedding projects take a bit more time and administrative effort than regular indexing projects. Per-page rates are hard to charge on embedded projects. The pages change all the time, so how do you count them? There is also additional work on your part to make sure that the process is clear, that you have the right files, that you have made arrangements for file transfer, and that your machine can handle the files once they arrive. Are special macros or add-on programs needed, something your client has developed especially for embedding indexing? Sometimes doing a quick test is a good idea, to make sure everything is working properly. Your overhead is higher, as you are running a bigger machine and expensive software. Trying to calculate all these extra activities into a per-page rate would be very hard. Hourly rates work much better and allow room for unforeseen problems such as file corruption and troubleshooting.

Be aware that some clients do not realize what is involved in embedding, and expect to offer the same per page rate as for traditional indexing. We just went through all the arguments against this approach, and it will be up to you to educate the client about what is involved. Only a highly experienced indexer working with an old and trusted client could work with a per page rate on these types of projects, This project must be very predictable, and all processes would have to be tested thoroughly to complete the project within those bounds. And embedding is just not predictable!

Make sure you have a strong contact at the client's office. Take the time to hammer out together explicit steps for the project. Be very clear about who has which files when, whom you turn things over to, whom you get files from, and how long you have to complete the project. Who has the "hot potato"? Make sure that what you are offering to do is clear (discussions on INDEX-L have revealed a variety of ways to work with clients). Some clients want their codes completely clean, others want you to edit only the compiled index and do not care about the codes. Be very clear about what you are providing, so that there are no misunderstandings later.

Your clients would probably appreciate a discussion of the pluses and minuses of embedding. Often, when shown how much more the index will cost, they are happy to live without embedding. But in many instances, embedding is the only option the production process will allow to achieve full use of the publication. It is cost-effective if the embedding can save time in translation, save time in conversion to online formats, or save time in the next version of the book.

Good luck if you decide to try it, and may your indexes always compile!

REFERENCES/RESOURCES

Books and Articles

Malik, Ed, "Indexing at Frame Technology Corporation" in "What Editors Need and Want: Are They Getting It?", *The Changing Landscapes of Indexing, The Proceedings of the 26th Annual Meeting of the American Society of Indexers*, San Diego, California, May 13-14, 1994, American Society of Indexers, 1994.

Mauer, Peg, "Embedded Indexing: What is It and How Do I Do It?" *Key Words*, 1998; Jan/Feb:14-15.

Mauer, Peg, "Embedded Indexing in FrameMaker," *Key Words*, 1998; Sept./Oct.:1, 6.

Mulvany, Nancy, *Indexing Books*, University of Chicago Press, 1994.

Tutorial

Maislin, Seth, "Tutorial on Index Tagging"
(http://www.oreilly.com/people/staff/seth/tutor.html)

Chapter 2

Indexing Computer-Related Documents

Lynn Moncrief © 1999

INTRODUCTION

The explosion in personal computing and in computer technology has brought a wealth of opportunities for indexers. Annually, traditional publishers produce numerous books on computer topics, while software and hardware companies constantly issue new products with manuals that require indexes. Indexers can find work with these high-technology publishers or can subcontract with technical documentation firms or with freelance technical writers.

The range of audiences for computer-related documents is wide and varied, as is the range of topics. These documents are not limited to end-user software manuals, but include programming, Internet, and networking topics among others. Hardware companies, in addition to computer manufacturers, are also a good potential source of clients. Many hardware products have a sizeable software component that requires its own set of indexed manuals. There are advantages and disadvantages to working with high-technology companies (and their contractors) vs. working with traditional publishers. It is simply a matter of personal taste which type of client you prefer. I have truly enjoyed working with both.

TRADITIONAL VS. NONTRADITIONAL PUBLISHERS

Payment Rates

High-technology companies usually pay higher rates than traditional publishers. If the index is to be embedded, per page rates are even higher. Some companies pay an hourly rate for indexing projects; and embedding, of course, requires many additional hours. (For more information on embedded indexing, see Chapter 1 by Jan Wright.)

Direct Contact with Authors

When dealing with high-technology companies, you are more likely to have direct access to authors. This creates an immeasurable advantage if questions arise. In fact, the author is often the primary contact person, especially when you are subcontracting to a freelance technical writer. In other cases, the project lead or a manager of the technical documentation department serves as the primary contact person and can put you in touch with the writer.

Positive interaction with the writers improves the quality of the index. Indexes to technical manuals are often produced under extremely challenging conditions. This holds true for all involved in the project, writers and indexers included. As long as the indexer keeps in mind that technical writers are invariably under intense deadline pressure and are facing their own challenges, they are almost always receptive to indexing questions.

Space for the Index

Space rarely, if ever, arises as an issue when creating indexes to technical documents published by high-technology companies. Usually, the manuals are soft-cover or in loose-leaf binders (a likely format for internal documents), and not bound into signatures like hardcover books published by traditional publishers. Space for the index becomes limited when the publisher does not want to add another signature to the book, allotting for the index only what is left over in the last signature. This allotment can lead to the ridiculous situation of having only 10 pages for an index to a highly technical 800-page book, i.e., a superficial index. The ability to index to the depth demanded by the document is one of the joys of indexing for high-technology companies. The only real negative pressure on index length comes from the extremely tight deadlines.

Indexing Concurrently with Document Development

Sometimes the text is still being written while indexing is in progress—not an ideal situation. This results in "chunking," which is receiving portions of the book in separate batches from the client. If you prefer to index the book in order from cover to cover, you'll find chunking a challenge (unless you have time to wait until you receive the entire book). I believe that many computer-related texts, especially software user manuals, can be indexed well out of sequence, leaving some questions pending the arrival of additional chapters.

Much more difficult is chunking out chapters of a book containing an embedded index. If a client insists on this, ask for all of the files when completed so that you will be able to edit the index tags embedded within them. Otherwise, you will be faced with editing the index on hard-copy and sending the complete list of edits to the client. Another problem with "chunking out" chapters is the enormous administrative overhead created by filling out airbills, running out to courier service dropoff boxes, etc., on a daily or near daily basis. You should be compensated for all of this additional effort. Of course, many publishers now accept emailed documents, which cuts down considerably on both cost and time.

Indexing a Moving Target

Another possible problem happens when the client simultaneously rewrites the chapters as you merrily index them. You are then asked to revise the index to incorporate the changes. This is not the writer's fault. In these situations, the author is dealing with a product that is still being tweaked by the engineers, so they too are working with a moving target. A good relationship with the project manager or the head of the technical documentation staff is essential in these cases because you then have to negotiate a higher fee. When this happened to me, the reorganization and rewrites had been so extensive that I had to index it again from scratch. The client agreed to pay me double the original fee.

Extreme Deadline Pressure

Deadline pressure can be worse with high-technology clients than with traditional publishers. This happens because product manual deadlines are tied to the product delivery date, and delays often occur in getting page proofs to the indexer. The high-technology industry is a pressure cooker for all involved. Usually development of the product itself has slipped a number of times and eventually the entire development team (including the documentation staff) runs up against the hard wall called *The End of the Quarter* by which the product (with manual) must ship. While this hectic scheduling is usually the norm, I have worked for software company clients with quite leisurely delivery schedules.

Slipping Delivery Dates

The client may call to schedule the indexing project months in advance, but is not ready to deliver the page proofs and/or files by the promised date. This can make scheduling a challenge. Because schedule slippage is a fact of life when working with software (and other high-tech companies), the indexer must be very flexible. I advise against turning down other projects to keep a block of time open for an anticipated delivery, unless the client has a very good history of timely delivery. Of course, this means that you often end up overloaded because when the project with the slipped schedule arrives, it inevitably collides with the other projects you lined up in the interim.

Embedded Indexes

High-technology companies and some traditional publishers require an embedded index. There are several points to consider in deciding whether you want to do embedded indexes. Embedded indexing is likely to require an investment on your part in additional software and possibly upgraded hardware unless you choose to embed only in the word processing software you already have. While some clients may require embedding in Microsoft Word, many prefer that the index be embedded in desktop publishing software, such as FrameMaker or PageMaker. These packages can be quite expensive, especially if purchased directly from their publishers. Desktop publishing software may also require the purchase of additional RAM and a larger hard drive. I do not recommend purchasing any software solely for the purpose of doing embedded indexes unless you have a firm commitment to projects from a client that will cover the expense of investing in it, or you are so wildly confident of your marketing skills that you are sure you will get projects requiring that particular software. Hidden hardware costs may include the need to purchase a high-capacity removable disk drive (e.g., a Zip drive) and a fast modem for making file transfers.

INDEXING TECHNIQUES

If you are familiar with standard indexing practices, you are well on your way to indexing computer books. Readers who are new to indexing should also take indexing courses and/or read the excellent works on the subject by Nancy Mulvany, Hans Wellisch, or Larry Bonura. (See References/Resources at end of this chapter.) These are all useful references for indexing computer-related documents and provide, as well, a good overview of indexing.

Indexing Manuals

The term "manuals" includes (but is not limited to) software manuals, programming manuals, Web site design texts, reference books, and related material. Readers of these texts are primarily interested in how to solve a given problem and, thus, the index should provide quick access to the needed information on the subject.

Handling Procedural Information

Most computer-related documents are full of procedures. While reading procedure after procedure can cause one's eyes to glaze, it is vitally important to read them in their entirety or learn to quickly scan them for indexable information. This scanning ability comes with experience.

Gerund-Object Approach

Well-organized books usually title their procedures. The appropriateness of the titles is another matter (one that you have to consider when deciding how to index a given procedure). The title of the procedure (or what *should* be the title) usually gives you a clue to how to index the procedure. If the procedure is titled inappropriately, you must read through the procedure and introductory information, if any, to determine accurately what task it describes. You must be aware that readers differ in how they try to find the information in the index. Consider the following:

A reader wants to find the procedure titled *Formatting Your Hard Disk*.

Reader A looks in the index for:
　hard disk
　　formatting
Reader B, on the other hand, looks for
　formatting
　　hard disk
Reader C might look under
　drives. *See* hard disk

Unless space is an issue, all of these permutations should appear in the index.

This brings us to the perennial debate in the indexing community over using verbs as main headings. Use of the gerund or noun form of a verb commonly appears in indexes to computer-related texts and is essential to producing a user-friendly index. While many users think of the object of the task they want to perform, many others first think of the task. Some indexers prefer to cast the entire concept, including object, as a main heading when indexing tasks under their gerund forms with the following results:

　formatting floppy disks *(or diskettes, if that is the usage in the text)*
　formatting hard disks

This is also perfectly acceptable, though I personally find it easier to scan indexes when the objects of the gerunds are listed as subentries. The above format becomes necessary, however, when clients forbid sub-subentries. It is also used, of course, when there is only one object (what would otherwise constitute a subentry) of the gerund.

I've indexed more than one book that not only described formatting disks and diskettes, but also formatting characters, paragraphs, etc. Personally, I preferred not to mix these types of concepts in one subentry list under a main heading that simply says *formatting*.

Keep in mind that computer users often are experiencing panic by the time they refer to the manual. Many do not like to use manuals and are already in high temper because the product's interface isn't intuitive enough to quickly figure out how to perform a given task. So by the time they pull the manual off the shelf, they are in no mood to go flipping through the index trying to second-guess the indexer. Therefore, when space allows, provide multiple access points for procedural information by also using the gerund form for main headings.

If space limitations prevent double-posting, I prefer indexing under the noun (e.g., "hard disk" as main entry with "formatting" as subentry) because the noun heading for the concept most likely will contain other subentries (e.g., "hard disk" as main heading with "surface errors" and "physical structure" as additional subentries).

It should go without saying, but some indexes compel me to say it: Main headings should never consist of adjectives or adverbs without the nouns or verbs they modify.

Do Not Over-Index

Determining what is or is not indexable *within* procedures can be difficult. Often, only the procedure as a whole is indexable. However, exceptions crop up. Do not index every step of the procedure. Not only is it unnecessary, but it can massively swell the index with trivial entries.

Often there is a temptation to index certain steps because they appear as paragraphs, representing mini-procedures in themselves. Only index these steps when the information contained in the step is not discussed more fully elsewhere in the book. The difficulty lies in determining whether that is the case. A good read or scan of the entire text prior to indexing will help you decide. If in doubt, index the "mini-procedure." If you later find it discussed more substantively, you can always delete the locator for the earlier reference.

In some texts, procedures contain boilerplate for a certain step that is repeated in many other procedures. Opening or saving files is an example. When you encounter boilerplate, do not index multiple instances of identical text. This can lead to long strings of locators. If you feel that you *must* index multiple instances of a procedural step, create subentries for the context in which they occur.

Indexing Warnings, Cautions, and Notes

These are often set off within a box or by a different font. You need to rely on your own judgment whether to index this type of information. I do not recommend creating a main heading for warnings, cautions, and notes as this can lead to long, classified lists (see below). However, if a warning or caution alerts the user to a potential loss of data, electrocution (in a hardware manual), or equipment damage, I index it under any heading that the reader is likely to scan. But watch out for boilerplate repetitions of these as well.

Tutorials

Many manuals contain tutorials, sometimes of great length. In fact, you can encounter entire manuals devoted to tutorials. Deciding whether and how to index these can be difficult. You may be tempted to create a main heading for the tutorial with a ranged locator spanning 50 pages, then move on to other things. Of course, you have to do much more analysis with a tutorial spanning 50 pages or an entire book. It helps to remember that some computer users actually work their way through tutorials.

Procedures are often mirrored or amplified in tutorials. It may be useful to make a subheading under the appropriate main heading that simply says "tutorial." I've created indexes with the following subheadings, among others:

    slide show presentations
       procedure
       tutorial

It may be tempting to skim tutorials because of their tediousness. If you must scan rather than read them, scan them with an eye for the procedures within them. Often, they contain multiple procedures and these instances (repetitions of procedures described elsewhere) should be indexed, if only with a locator. Some lengthy tutorials are presented like case studies in marketing and other texts. If they have a company or some other name describing the project covered in the tutorial, I recommend creating a main heading for the name followed by the term "tutorial." For example, if a software suite manual has lengthy tutorials about how to create a slide show presentation for ABC, Inc., along with other projects, I'd create the following entries:

ABC, Inc. tutorials
  brochures
  newsletter
  slide show presentation
slide show presentations
  ABC, Inc. tutorial *(or simply tutorial, unless there are others)*
  procedure
  XYZ, Inc. tutorial

Some users who work through the tutorials in separate sessions want to find the section they were working through (such as the slide show presentation) in the index. Do not assume that all users would look under the heading for the procedure itself. Some users may access it under the name of the fictional company. If the entire book is a tutorial, do not list individual procedures under tutorial as a main heading.

Graphical User Interface (GUI) Components

GUI components consist of menu bars and their menus, pop-up menus, toolbars and their buttons, windows (with their scrollbars, status bars, etc.), dialog boxes with their buttons, dropdown boxes, combination boxes, check boxes, and radio buttons. In a reasonably well-organized and clearly written text, the hierarchies of these components should be readily discernable. However, this is not always the case, and you may have to read very carefully or even study accompanying screen shots to determine what is going on. If you don't have screen shots (or a recent version of the software) available, you may need to go back to the project manager and ask for this type of documentation.

One problem frequently arises with identically named GUI components. A software suite likely has "File," "Edit," "Insert," and "Tool" menus for each component application, yet the menu items under each could differ. The index should be clear about which component application a menu belongs to. For example, if you were indexing a book about *Perfect Office* with substantive discussions about certain commands under the "Insert" menu, the index should contain an entry similar to the following:

Insert menu
  File command (WordPerfect), 3.18
  Import command (Presentations), 2.28

Many software manuals describe menu items (also called menu commands or menu choices) in a substantive manner. Paragraphs devoted to describing them should be indexed, while passing mentions should not. They should be double-posted under the main headings for the menus they belong to and as separate main headings. For example, the excellent index to *Special Edition Using Windows 95* (Que, 1995), which lists Mary Jane Frisby and Kathy Venable as the indexers, contains the following entry:

Object command (Insert menu)
    OLE, 411, 440
    WordPad (Paint), 397-407

This command is dutifully double-posted as:

Insert menu commands
    Object (OLE), 411, 440
    Object (Paint), 397-407

Determining the depth of indexing of these components can create a challenge. As with any type of topic, whether these components are discussed substantively is key to determining whether to index them.

Dialog boxes pose a particular problem requiring designation as main headings. You can find yourself in a hopeless wallow if you start indexing the individual components within dialog boxes. The temptation to index individual buttons, list boxes, and other components arise when the author discusses them in some detail as part of the dialog box containing them. Unless the text is a programming manual describing how to actually create these components (often called controls), or the author expounds at length about specific controls, omit them from the index. If you index them as main headings, you'll fill the index with trivial entries that readers most likely don't need. Nor is it necessary to index them as subentries under the main heading for the dialog box since that would create a listing of subentries all referring to the same small range of page numbers. Subentry lists for dialog boxes, if any, should contain entries for performing various tasks within the dialog boxes (if the author discusses them again elsewhere).

Inconsistent nomenclature happens often enough to merit discussion. In poorly edited texts, the same GUI component is referred to by slightly different names. Screen shots become your best friend here in determining which variant to use. Remember that the reader often has the software on the screen and will refer to the component in the index by whatever appears in the title bar of the dialog box or other component.

INDEXING PROGRAMMING TEXTS

The issues described above also apply to programming texts; however, there are a few topics peculiar to these documents.

Blocks of Program Code (Code Blocks)

It is unnecessary to index individual lines of code, although it is useful to create entries for the task performed by the sample code listing. Code blocks can take up ten to twenty pages, so you can't just go whizzing blithely by without paying homage in the index. The purpose of a code block is not always immediately obvious, especially if the code block does not have an explanatory heading. In these instances, you will need to do a close reading of the text surrounding the code block.

If, for some reason, you must read the code block itself, look for *comment* lines. Comments are explanatory lines, not executable code. In most languages (including C and C++), comment lines are preceded by a semi-colon (;). Because you can usually get away with creating one or two entries that cover a huge code block, fairness to the publisher may dictate deducting these sections from the indexable page count when invoicing. However, if you must go digging into the code itself, by all means charge for those pages. In any case, you should at least scan these pages for separate indexable routines (often set off by headings).

Programming Language Components

Identify the type of component (statement, function, construct, loop, etc.) in the index. I stress this because I have seen indexes where they weren't unidentified, with confusing results. (This also holds true for GUI components.) Watch for multiple language components bearing the same name. The ugly twins are often "statements"/"functions" and "events"/"messages." Function names in most programming or scripting languages are followed by a set of parentheses. Thus, you can have:

Get statement

Get( ) function

Unfortunately, some writers neglect to indicate whether they mean the statement or the function of the same name. When it is unclear whether a statement or a function is being referred to, remember that functions retrieve values (hence the parentheses). If you still can't tell what is going on from the text, read any code samples within the discussion. If you find the name of the language component immediately followed by a variable name within parentheses (no space), you are dealing with a function.

To keep from making this too easy, not all function names are followed by the set of parentheses. *Member* functions have the following format:

CArchive::Read member function

CList::Serialize member function

The word before the double colon is the name of the class of which the function (following the colons) is a *member*. Be sure to adhere to the typographical conventions and syntactical rules of the language when writing entries for language components.

Object-Oriented Programming Horrors

When indexing OOP (object-oriented programming) texts, clearly identify the following, easily confused components correctly:

methods

instance methods

class instances

class instance methods

class methods

Note that the above items are not arranged alphabetically, but do form the neat mental circle they create. (Even if I didn't have a point to make with that, it was fun to do.)

HTML Tags

The two major problems associated with indexing HTML tags are toggles and sorting tag names. Toggles are pairs of tags, such as the <CAPTION> and </CAPTION> tags. Usually, they are discussed together in the text and can be combined in an index heading as:

<CAPTION> and </CAPTION> tags

Note that the tag names appear in angle brackets (< >). Be sure to set your indexing program to force the sort on the first letter of the tag name. Readers will not find them if the entries all float to the top of the index and are included among the symbols.

ISSUES COMMON TO COMPUTER-RELATED TEXTS

To Classify or Not

Classifying is listing similar items as subentries under a higher level heading in a hierarchy of concepts (as in the Dewey Decimal System or genus-species relationships). For example, to list every menu by name under a main heading "menus" is classifying. Unless you have only a few subentries, do not fall into this trap. The problems that can be caused by classifying include: generating subentry lists that may span several columns or even pages; forcing what would otherwise be subentries to become subsubentries; not including every possible item in the list; and developing idiosyncratic or non-intuitive classification schemes. Under main headings that tempt you to classify—"dialog boxes," "controls," "methods,"—list only those items that apply to most or all of the items of that type. Here is how I handled the heading for "menu commands" in a text on PageMaker:

menu commands. *See also specific menu commands; menus*
    Story vs. Layout Editor, 259-260
    types of, 25-26

The *specific menu commands and menus*, of course, are indexed by title as main headings. This does not mean that you should never classify. Nancy Mulvany, in *Indexing Books* (pp. 73-75), gives an excellent description of situations when it could be useful. Whether you classify or not, post these items also as main headings.

Acronyms

Computer-related texts make an alphabet soup of acronyms. The standard rules for double-posting acronyms apply to these texts. Some acronyms have become so common, however, that individuals rarely look for them under their spell-outs. In these circumstances, double-posting seems ludicrous. After having secretly broken the double-posting rule for these in my own indexes, I finally admitted to doing so on INDEX-L. I was relieved to find out that other indexers have also stopped religiously double-posting in these instances. For example: RAM (random access memory) and PC (personal computer) systems. Whether to double-post a given acronym requires a judgment call, and you will not be condemned for not double-posting the very common ones.

Initial Capital Letters

Using initial capital letters in main headings can create havoc with the usability of computer-related texts. Case helps in readily distinguishing between commands, GUI components, and program components. Initial caps can significantly slow index-scanning speed, especially when language syntax is case-sensitive. If you are working for a publisher who specifies initial caps in their style guide, try to dissuade them from this practice in indexes to computer-related texts.

Symbols and Numbers

As with indexes to other types of texts, symbols and numbers should be sorted at the very top of the index, before letter group A. Numbers, as in other texts, should also be double-posted at their spellouts. Double-post symbols according to the format shown in the following example:

+ (plus sign)
    as addition operator
    as concatenation operator
plus sign (+)
    as addition operator
    as concatenation operator

While numbers should be sorted in ascending order at the beginning of the index, there is no clear-cut standard for sorting symbols. Let your indexing software take care of this for you as few readers know the ASCII values of various characters (which has been recommended for governing the sort order of symbols). Fortunately, the listing of symbols usually remains short and easy to scan.

In programming texts (including texts containing HTML tags), some component names are preceded with a symbol. The name of the language component should be sorted on the first letter, not the leading symbol(s). For example, the entry _UNI-CODE symbol should be sorted on UNICODE as shown in the following example:

UINT variables, 179-180
Unicode APIs, 314-320
UNICODE strings, 160-161, 203-207
_UNICODE symbol, 315
UNIX systems. *See also* Motif; Motif widgets; Wind/U tool
    byte swapping in RISC, 187

REFERENCES

Bonura, Larry, *The Art of Indexing*. New York: John Wiley and Sons, Inc., 1994.

Mulvany, Nancy, *Indexing Books*. Chicago: The University of Chicago Press, 1994.

Wellisch, Hans, *Indexing from A to Z*. New York: H.W. Wilson, 1995.

Part 2
Beyond the Book:
Web Indexing

Chapter 3

Subject-Oriented Web Indexing

Dwight Walker

INTRODUCTION

My goal in this short article is to bring you up to speed on Web indexing. I assume you are a person with good word skills and an inquisitive mind. Also, I assume you have good keyboard skills, access to the Internet, and have already created some HTML pages using, say, Netscape Composer. You may need help from your Internet Service Provider (ISP) to upload pages onto your Web site. This article is based on my experience teaching an online interactive course in Web indexing for my company, WWWalker Web Development, in 1998. We develop Web sites, support Linux and Windows NT, write technical articles, and specialize in Web indexing.

SEARCHING THE INTERNET

Most people who have used the Internet for any length of time know how hard it is to find information quickly. Search engines provide thousands of hits in response to a basic query, and it would take days to go through all the entries to find what you are seeking. Similarly, it can take ages to surf through related links to find information by chance.

To address this problem, people have started creating lists of favorite links and putting them online. These lists function as Web indexes. Increasingly, in newsletters, magazines, and newspapers, editors supply valuable links along with short commentaries and site addresses. Many people appreciate accessing information provided by an informed intermediary, rather than trusting technology to solve the problem of finding useful information.

Humans play an extremely important role in the information economy. Faster PCs, bigger screens, or quicker modems do not, in themselves, enhance productivity. Using research skills or hiring a researcher to find information is more vital than it ever was. Because the medium has changed and people can access so much information from their homes, wherever in the world they reside, there is a snowballing need to share information among people who live in different countries and speak different languages.

If you know how to build Web indexes, you can gain access to customers on the other side of the world and serve them in the comfort of their own homes. Barriers to entry are being ripped down. A vast amount of information, in a large array of formats, is "published" daily for international distribution. Authors are loading books; performers are loading audio and video clips; teenagers are loading games; database consultants are loading knowledge bases; newspaper and magazine editors are loading articles and excerpts; and there are ever increasing numbers of Internet-dedicated e-zines, email newsletters, and Web news sites.

Most people do not have the skills, time, or interest needed to effectively classify information. Indexers and librarians do and can apply their word and information classification skills in this lively Internet environment. Most indexers and librarians, however, do not know how to transfer skills derived from working with books and magazines to the world of online information. They are familiar with page numbers. Now, librarians and indexers work with URLs (Universal Resource Locators); they are used to scanning finite pages of text, now they may be working with long, undifferentiated columns of text, with JPEG images, or MPEG sound files.

How you might develop and market these new skills is limited only by your imagination. If you have specialized knowledge about Persian carpets, for instance, you can provide a service to manufacturers by listing all the materials, suppliers, and market information the manufacturers or their customers might access by surfing the Web. You can build up a database of valuable links on this topic. Manufacturers might pay you to access this list or pay you a monthly retainer to keep the list up to date. The competition is getting hotter and, for many people trying to distinguish themselves from the crowds, a Web index is essential.

AUSTRALIAN SOCIETY OF INDEXERS WEB INDEXING PRIZE

In 1996 when I was Webmaster of the Australian Society of Indexers (AusSI), I started to think the Web could be classified like a back of book style index and allow quick and easy access to information. I ran the AusSI Web Indexing Prize starting in 1996. The first year there were a handful of advanced indexes and a few simple ones. The second year there were many sophisticated Web databases and annotated indexes. Usually the entries were annotated lists of links. The third year, many more indexers used databases and meta data to classify their information. Sometimes people would spend the time to cull out by hand the worthless links and compile the most relevant links. Other times people would use databases to classify and collect the data. The audience dictated what was listed and how the Web site was designed.

The first-place winners for 1996-1998 were Alan Wilson's Australian Parliamentary Library Index (1996); Christabel Wescombe's University of Sydney Library

Education Internet Guide (1997); and Lloyd Sokvitne's Tasmania Online (1998). Liz Holliday was the manager of the manual subject index for Tasmania Online, and Elizabeth Louden was the cataloguer. See details on the AusSI Web site.

CHANGING APPROACHES TO WEB INDEXING

Since I started researching this area in 1996, Web indexing has come to mean many things. First, it was a virtual library of topic-related links to sites on the Web at large. Later, people began uploading online books and bibliographies that could be accessed through the Web. This led to database-driven Web indexes. And individual Web sites were themselves growing ever larger, so people needed to create Web site indexes to the internal contents of the site. Intranets have spawned the need to tie several Web servers into a central index so that staff can find information wherever it is stored. Some examples of Web indexes and Web index design can be found on the AusSI Web site.

CLASSIFYING AND NAMING LINKS

The association of ideas is fundamental to Web indexing. The Web, as its name implies, is founded on associations, each thread connected to another through some similarity or complementary attribute. But free association, though powerful and often entertaining, can be frustrating and, eventually, the need for classification systems arise.

One of the earliest classification systems to appear on the Web was Yahoo's hierarchical index. It provided broad categories that allowed people to find information quickly on specific topics. More informal classification systems developed as people converged into online "neighborhoods" clustered around topical home pages where discussion lists and focused information exchanges could occur. Despite its enormous size and essentially anarchic structure, the Web has managed to meet a need for immediate information and has been very easy to customize at very little cost. Today, there are whole swags of game sites, news sites, hobbyist pages, or sites for political activists. Every niche can be catered to, and that is where indexing becomes especially important.

THESAURI

A thesaurus is a controlled vocabulary for a particular field of information, similar to a huge information map with broader, narrower, and related terms in a maze of relationships. For high-end Web indexing, a thesaurus can be used to encode pages or insert index terms into an index consistently. The browser can then funnel down the Web-based thesaurus to find appropriate information. Thesauri can help mesh the different views of users as they search for information on a Web site.

For example, an astronomy index was needed for a large archive of information on stars. The images would be indexed using the correct astronomical term. Cross-references from popular names to the scientific terms would be available. Galaxies and nebulae could also be explored from this Web-based thesaurus index, allowing people to troll through the vast stores of information in an image database. Commercial software, such as MultiTes (www.concentric.net/~multites) makes creating thesauri much easier than in the past. MultiTes thesauri can be loaded onto the Web and integrated with your Web index.

While people have begun to recognize the importance of naming links in understandable ways, many still have bizarre or arcane names (e.g., extensive numeric URLs), and it is the indexer's job to rename these links in the index to make the meaning more clear. As in book indexing, indexers can double-post and put that link in more than one place.

To get the most out of Web indexing, you need to appreciate the transience and changeability of the readers. If you place your email address on your index, you will receive feedback on whether the index works or not, unlike paper-based indexes that allow no feedback to the indexer. This has moved the focus away from the book to the index as the key to information in the online world. Publishers cannot just load their books online and hope people will get better value out of them. They need indexers to work with Web site designers to help people access the books. Publishers and authors need indexes more than ever because of the myriad ways people have stored information in this huge conglomerate system.

LEARNING WEB INDEXING

I taught online interactive Web indexing classes for several months in 1998. In those classes I had students build an index based on a topic or create an index of a Web site from a particular viewpoint. I asked my students to produce an index to a site that had no index, or for an online book catalogue. This gave indexers practical experience indexing using HTML instead of paper. They also learned to design their index to interact with the document to which it refers. A common mistake was to just use the name of the page the Web site had given to a page. Students were taught to rename these links so that the name reflected the topic indexed.

Another goal of the course was to develop searching skills in order to create lists of references (i.e., identify appropriate URLs to add to the index). Many students needed to learn search skills. We would go over, say, a hunt for links to "London" only to find most of the returns from Alta Vista were businesses, when what we were looking for was tourist information. We had to abandon that broad approach.

"Australian rock musicians" was a sufficiently narrow topic to get only a few hits and not so much dross, so I asked one student to build an index to that topic.

Then I moved into <META> tagging. We inserted Dublin Core <META> tags into the top of Web pages to help search engines be able to better retrieve them. (See Marilyn Rowland's article "<META> Tags" Chapter 7.) These tags are used to specify the creator, date, publisher, and other information about the Web site. The National Library of Australia developed a Java tool called Reggie to take cataloguing codes and insert them into the correct <META> tags. This data was then pasted into the HTML page.

As is often the case, we would start out with grandiose schemes, such as trying to index an online bookshop's catalogue, only later realizing we had to have our HTML tags right or they would not work. I would look at the student's work and edit it and upload it to our class site so they could all look at it. They would come back with exclamations—"oh, so that's how you indexed that topic!" It was great to see the collaboration.

One of the weaknesses of human indexing is inconsistency; people often index the same material in more than one way. I did not opt for a thesaurus back then to control the vocabulary. I also did not prevent students from using their own style of indexing. Some were wordy, others put in annotations, while others just input a keyword with several links beside it. The main idea was to see how they approached the information. I could see they often had a particular bent in indexing. Some were very academic and would put in endless subheadings. Others would spend more time and devise more links by surfing down large sites with already accumulated links and reorganizing them into their own genre.

I tried to encourage them to index at least 20 links on a topic to make it cover sufficient ground. It is very easy to waste endless amounts of time in this field just surfing. I spent over 20 hours in January 1998 judging the 1997 Web indexing prize! Some of the sites had links to links to links. I would get totally lost!

Since the end of my course, the idea of an alphabetic Web index has become more and more popular with library schools, where they are called subject gateways. This is only one of the many forms of Web indexing. (See Seth Maislin's article, "Ripping Out the Pages," Chapter 5.)

HTML

HTML is a simplified version of SGML (Standard Generalized Markup Language). This is a set of tags that provide content and layout information for a document. For example:

<H1>Main Heading</H1> is a level 1 heading with the words Main Heading. The basic link HTML code is:

<A HREF="http://www.abc.com/">ABC</A>

This will let the browser jump from the word ABC on a Web page to a another Web site called www.abc.com using the HTTP protocol. You cannot edit an external Web document to insert anchors (tags in the document that allow you to jump to a point, not just to the top of the page). See below for more on anchors.

LINKS AND THE DEPTH OF INDEXING

Web indexing has several down sides. One is that the Web changes all the time. A link that worked one week may disappear the next. It is wise, then, to know a little about link construction in case you have to work in HTML to repair your index. The maintenance of links is very time-consuming. The hypertext world does not contain page numbers. To access a piece of information you need to know its URL and create a link to that URL.

Let's take a closer look at URLs. The Internet is a massive computer network composed of millions of nodes. To communicate between nodes, each machine is given a unique number or IP (Internet Protocol) address, e.g., 203.15.68.8. To avoid having to remember the weird number combination that comprises IP addresses, *domain names* were introduced. The above number may be better known as the domain name: www.zeta.org.au. Each domain name has a corresponding IP address. So if you typed in: http://203.15.68.8/, it is the same Web site as http://www.zeta.org.au. The Domain Name Server (DNS) converts the domain name into the IP address by accessing a huge database. This means that if you use a domain name, rather than an IP address, in your index, your index link will not break if the machine is changed or the site is moved. The URL serves as your "electronic page number."

To construct the location of a piece of information on the Internet, you specify the protocol (http://) followed by the domain (www.zeta.org.au), then the directory (/~aussi/webindexing/), followed by the file name (links.htm), followed by an anchor within the page (#subject-oriented lists) (including the space) to give the URL:

http://www.zeta.org.au/~aussi/webindexing/links.htm#subject-oriented lists

This will point us, for example, to a paragraph on a page sitting on the Zeta Web Server—a good bibliography of Web indexes. To provide access to it, insert this URL in your index.

ANCHORS—JUMPING WITHIN A PAGE

Another problem indexers encounter with HTML is that it may be hard for the user to locate information in a large page if the page does not include specific anchors. Often, viewers can use the Find button on the top of the browser to sift through the information. Normally indexers cannot add anchor tags to an external site's HTML, so they are limited to jumping to the top of the page only, not halfway down as you would in a book index using, say, paragraph numbers. Traditional book indexers kept pushing toward this design as if to extend their prowess onto the HTML world the same as they did in the book world.

Because of the transient nature of the Web, I tend to avoid indexing to the anchor level. For online books this is not a problem, but there is still a need for a visual depth indicator on the Web page to help readers get their bearings, e.g., Yahoo's hierarchical guide at the top of their pages. The trouble with hypertext is that people very quickly get lost. Jumping around may be fun for programmers, but it can be tiring and distracting for users. I try to talk new would-be indexers out of indexing too deeply too early. In my first few courses, we would spend hours getting the HTML kinks worked out of indexes that used anchors. In the end, students learned how to index to an appropriate depth.

Building Web databases would be a better choice if you need great specificity. It takes time to encode a Web database and this may not be as interactive as a free-form index but it works. The same applies to image maps and other forms of HTML magic. Although it looks good, it requires a good tool and know-how to set up the Web server; otherwise, leave well enough alone.

When you are indexing within a Web site, use relative links. If the files for the site are in a single directory, all the links in your index can be just the file name, e.g., productX.html, instead of the full URL (or absolute link): http://www.abc.com/productX.html. This won't change the way the links function, but it will give you cleaner HTML, allow you to work offline more easily, and allow you to move your Web site and its associated index to another directory or domain in the future without having to recode the index.

SEARCH ENGINES AND FEEDBACK

You need to learn how to use a search engine effectively, both to find information to add to your index and to increase the number of hits to your site. The best approach to find relevant information involves starting with keywords chosen for specificity and then working backwards if you get no hits. Use your common sense as you scroll through what you retrieved and watch for juicy sites. Often, shopping sites or online bulletin board sites flood your results because they have coded key words into their headers. Look at the source code and see what meta tags appear in the page to explain why the page you picked up was retrieved. You may find a more appropriate keyword to search on than the one you originally tried. You can then refine your search to get better results.

To improve the number of hits to your index site, add a counter on it. Counters tell you the number of times people visit your site; knowing that you have received very few hits will encourage you to refocus or redistribute your site. I recommend putting <META> tags in your index page. If you get more and more hits to your index, you know you are on the right track. You can also identify where your hits are coming from through statistical tracking methods that may be offered by your server or ISP. You may find that 50% of your hits come from Australia, 30% from the U.S., and 20% from Europe. Make your URL more widely known by distributing it via mailing lists or feeding it into a search engine. Leave an email address for contact. You will be able to modify your index to suit your readership.

REAL LIFE APPLICATIONS

Toward the end of a course, I am usually peppered with questions about how people can make money doing this form of indexing. As was true with book indexing, there are no easy answers. Often people wish to save costs on their Web site so they don't want to pay to have it indexed. Large government departments or corporations are more likely to see the need for classifying. More and more in Australia, meta data is being used to aid retrieval.

Online technical writing also begs for online indexing skills. Technical writers frequently do not know about indexing, cross-references, classification, or retrieval. Looking for Web sites that are complex and have a flexible Webmaster is a good first step. There are also major password-protected online encyclopedias always hunting for links to go into their sites. You could work for them as a freelancer. Programmers will try to design a tool, such as a search engine, to replace the indexer. Instead, try working with the programmers in the design stage of a new Web database, using your database and information management skills to pick out fields and codes and help set up a really useful information site. People get sick of slick tricks in Java and HTML. What they really want are easy-to-use self-serve guides.

Unfortunately many users think access to information on the Internet should be "free," so the general public dislikes the idea of paying for information (I might be wrong here), but more and more businesses will pay for your expertise if you can show time savings for retrieving information. I did this for a company where I previously worked, called CEASA, on economics and mining resources. I produced about 300 links that I grouped into categories. People hitting the site ranged from universities to government departments to students. We used the list of links to benefit both our customers and ourselves. I used links such as CIA World Fact Book to do research, and our customers used it as a self-serve library, which saved them emailing us for free information. As a result, we saved research and customer service costs.

Remember, too, we are not limited to indexing text. We can index images, sounds, and software. Software remains abundantly available on the Web. Many large download archives (Download.com, for instance) do not provide very good indexing systems. If a shareware developer knew that a good index would help sales, I predict he would pay you to index his entry on a large download archive. The archive owner would probably index their product databases if the software developers who loaded their software saw the benefits in sales to them! With these areas growing, you will have a larger and larger base of online indexing work. I can also see indexing online newspapers a very useful, never-ending business. I believe "7am News on the Net" indexes all the Australian, New Zealand, and UK newspapers online for free in return for advertising. They supply a free Java ticker that people can add to their site. It lists the latest stories and lets the reader jump to the newspaper at the click of a mouse.

You may receive lots of little jobs through your Web site. You may invent a Web site from which people can search and buy information in the form of an index. You may receive a monthly retainer from a large Web publisher. You may get paid by the hour for searching for a business client. Be flexible. You don't have to be limited to current existing publishers either, as they are trying very hard to limit the slide of readers to the Web by launching their own Web pages. They may be your main competitors. Be wary of others in your same field, including fellow technical writers, librarians, publishers, whether Australians or North Americans! You may need to take your services to the Web at large. Don't be limited by your 9-to-5 job. You can do this indexing at home as moonlighting! See how it grows. If you get more and more business, you can open shop.

Don't think someone will pay for your index just because it is there. You need to get hold of the Webmaster and see what is being developed for the company and help them envision how your services will fit in. It will take some time to get your name on the hot list. Maybe end users will buy from you. Often the business sector is years behind because of old equipment and poorly managed technology transfer. Be part of the growing number of small business operators who are developing their own Web-based businesses. Set up a Web site for your business—many ISPs give you Web space (5-10 MB) as part of your email account. Geocities provides free Web space in return for a watermark (i.e., a reference to their service on your Web site— *see*, for example, Geocities.com). Get two or three pages up and samples of your work online. You may start getting some feedback. From there you can build an online-only clientele.

The sky is the limit.

REFERENCES

Articles

Australian Library and Information Association newsletter. See http://www.alia.org.au/incite/wwww/9902. html for an article by Kerry Webb about the Web Indexing Prize.

Walker, Dwight. "AusSI Web Indexing Prize" *The Indexer*. 1997 20(1):6-7

Walker, Dwight. "Web Indexing: An Exercise in Hypertext Navigation" *LASIE*, 1996, 27(3):50-58.

Walker, Dwight. "Web Indexing Prize 1997" *The Indexer*, 1997, 20(2).

Walker, Dwight. "Web Indexing—The State of Play" *Online Currents*, 1998, 13(2).

Web Sites

ANSI/IS'S Guidelines for the Construction, Format and Management of Monolingual Thesauri, ANSI/IS's Guidelines are not online, but are available for $49 from IS'S Press, Box 1056, Bethesda, MD 20827. For more information, see: http://www.niso.org/pubpub.html.

Australian Society of Indexers (AusSI) Web site, http://www.zeta.org.au/~aussi/.

CEASA (Commercial Economic Advisory Service of Australia), http://www.geko.net. au/~ceasa/. An Australian business information site.

Download.com, http://www.download.com/. A major source for freeware and shareware.

Dublin Core Metadata Initiative, http://purl.org/dc/. Information about efforts to standardize approaches to information retrieval on the Internet.

MultiTes, http://www.multites.com/. Commercial software for thesaurus construction.

7am News on the Net, http://www.7am.com/. An excellent source for international news.

Web Thesaurus Compendium, http://www-cui.darmstadt.gmd.de/~lutes/thesauri.html Contains links to numerous online thesauri.

WWWalker Web Development, http://www.wwwalker.com.au/.

Chapter 4

Web Indexing—Anchors Away!

Kevin Broccoli &
Gerry Van Ravenswaay © 1999

In this chapter we turn to embedded indexing for the Internet, frequently called Web indexing. We will define Web indexes; describe the structure of entries for Web indexes; present some of the challenges that Web indexers face; and compare Web indexes to search engines.

One of the difficulties in defining Web indexes is their relative newness. The first pages were placed on the World Wide Web in 1991 when Tim Berners Lee, its founder, uploaded four files. We are in a period of transition, moving from using well-established forms of writing and communications to others that are still in their infancy. Paramount among these is the Web. For indexers, this is an uncharted voyage where we must jettison firmly established ideas while developing new ones. Where the voyage will end is anyone's guess.

DEFINING WEB INDEXES

There are characteristics that indexes on Web sites share with print indexes. The goal of any index, as Henry Benjamin Wheatley stated, is to "bring together all the items on a similar subject which are separated in the book itself" (p. 59). Indexes are essentially lists; however, as we all know, there are many types of lists. According to the *Merriam Webster Dictionary*, for example, bibliographies are "lists often with descriptive or critical notes of writings related to a particular subject, period, or author." Catalogs are lists of items arranged systematically with descriptive details. Traditionally, indexes are alphabetical listings of the proper nouns, names, and topics that result from analyzing the content of a particular document.

On the Web, the term "index" has developed a broader, more general meaning. Frequently, one encounters "indexes" that are essentially a collection of URLs designed to take users to other Web sites. These Web sites can be collected manually, by search engines, or by spiders. There usually is little content analysis of the Web sites themselves. These types of lists are more like catalogs than they are like traditional indexes. However, with careful selection and annotation they can be much more (*See* Chapter 3, Dwight Walker, "Subject-Oriented Web Indexing").

Although there are numerous methods of organizing information in an index, Web indexes are usually arranged alphabetically. To organize information in other ways (e.g., by time or category) is to classify it, and as Wheatley stated in his seminal work, "We want as little classification as possible in an alphabetical index" (p.135).

PARTS OF A WEB INDEX ENTRY

Like print indexes, each entry in a Web index always contains at least two parts: the *headword* or *entry*, and the *locator*. Whereas the locator in print indexes is usually the page number, the locator in Web indexes is the name of the file and/or the name of an *anchor*. The anchors are placed by using the <A> and </A> HTML tags. The anchors are *inter* and *intra* document links that use two types of attributes following the first <A> code. The first, the HREF attribute (the header reference), takes the user from the entry in the index to the second, NAME attribute (locator reference) that directs users to the location of the information that they are seeking. The indexer must always create those two attributes and insert code identifying them. The file containing the index will consist of the HREF attributes. The NAME attributes will be placed by the indexer throughout the various documents that are being indexed.

An example of the coding for a Web index entry is presented below:

Borko, Harold, <A HREF="bibliog.htm#borkoA">1</A>

In this Web index entry, the HREF attribute "bibliog.htm" is Web page name referring to the entry. "#borkoA" identifies the point in the Web page where an anchor has been inserted. The number "1" is the locator. On the Web page, the locator will be underlined to identify it as the link to information about Harold Borko.

The code below shows how the Borko information on the bibliog.htm page is identified with a NAME attribute to create an anchor.

<P><B><A NAME="borkoA">Borko</A>, Harold</B> and <B>Charles L. Bernier</B><I>Indexing Concepts and Methods.</I> New York: Academic Press, 1978. ISBN 0121186601. </P>

Other tags shown in this example are <P></P> tags to set off paragraphs, <B></B> tags to create bold text, and <I></I> tags to create italic text.

A Web index at its simplest is a collection of these entries listed in alphabetical order and coded in HTML (Hypertext Markup Language). HTML is a formatting language, *not* a programming language. It is similar to early word processing programs that required you to place codes in the text to tell the computer how you wanted the text to appear in print. An example of the HTML coding for a Web index is presented below:.

BookWire Index of Publishers, <A href="publish.htm#bkwire"></A>

Borko, Harold, <A href="bibliog.htm#borkoA"></A>
Botanical Glossary, <A href="refbooks.htm#botanicalglos"></A>
Botanical Name Roots Dictionary, <A href="refbooks.htm#botroot"></A>
botany reference sources, <A HREF="refbooks.htm#zoo"></A>
Boulder Writers Alliance, <A HREF="orgpub.htm#bwa"></A>
Bradbury, Malcom, <A HREF="bibfiction.htm#bradbury"></A>
Brathwaite, Maria, <A HREF="chapters.htm#oh"></A>
In this example, <BR> tags are used to create line breaks.

CHALLENGES IN WEB INDEXING

Indexing Web sites presents numerous challenges. One is the timeliness of the information to be indexed. All information has a shelf life—some information has a longer shelf life than others. If the information on the Web site will be refreshed (updated) frequently, it will be difficult to keep the index current. For example, consider a Web page dedicated to the "Employee of the Month." The index will have to be refreshed monthly. It would be better to create an entry for "Employee of the Month," rather than use an employee's name that will need to be changed every month. It should be noted, however, that developing an index that requires regular updating and maintenance may not only be more interesting to the users of the site (i.e., the employees and their friends who will appreciate seeing their names in print) but adds to the possibility of additional work for the indexer.

Another special concern is download time. For print indexes, length is often a consideration because of the limited number of pages available. For Web indexes, length is measured in terms of the time required for the user to download the index and use it. If an index takes too long to download, it will not be used. Online users are notorious for having little patience.

One major factor that makes writing Web indexes difficult is the nature of the documents themselves. Whereas books are linear, electronic documents are non-linear. For example, electronic documents can be hierarchical. The information may be scattered throughout the site. In these situations, the index is critical for pulling all the information together. It becomes the gateway to the site. In Web indexes there are no page ranges so it is difficult to distinguish between extensive and cursory treatments of a subject.

Another challenge is multiple references. In print documents, these are easy to present; it is much harder online. There are several options. Headings or subheadings can be repeated with underlining indicating they are hot links. Another method is to have numbers or letters after the headings or subheadings indicating the frequency. However, if the screen is too full of lines, the index will not be visually appealing and an impatient user will not take the time to sift through it. Although screen technology is improving rapidly, Web indexes that contain great detail are more difficult to browse through and use. This is one reason that it is rare to find paragraph style indexes or indexes that have a large numbers of subentries.

Of course, while overcoming these challenges, you must remember that a successful Web index is measured by how quickly users can get in and out of the index page and find the desired information. The faster the user can get in, find the information, and go to the document, the better the index.

WEB INDEXES AND SEARCH ENGINES

One of the most frequently asked questions regarding Web indexes is "Why can't you use search engines instead?" Perhaps you have had the following experience. You visit a Web site, hoping to find information on a subject. You type a word or two into the site's search engine. What happens? Nothing is found! You try again, this time using a different term. Now you have results, but too many! You begin looking through the documents one at a time. After hours spent scanning many pages of text, you finally find what you're looking for.

All search engines do is scan text looking for occurrences of whatever letters you type into the search box interface. They then list every document containing those letters. Naturally, there are variations among individual search engines. Some do a free-text search, while others scan meta-data, and others scan only the headings of Web pages. Regardless of the search method, the results usually leave much to be desired. Either you are confronted with no results (because you didn't think of the exact word that the text used) or you access too many documents with irrelevant information

The primary benefit of an index over a search engine is the same as that of a book index over a concordance. The user is only led to information that directly relates to the search because the text has been analyzed by a trained, human indexer. The indexer has gone through a site line-by-line and made sure that the user will only be led only to useful information. Also, the indexer has created synonyms to take the user to the terms used by the author if the user has chosen an alternate term. Furthermore, the indexer has created entries for terms that are not directly stated in the text although the concept is implied. So far, no search engine has been created that can do that!

CONCLUSION

In reality, there is no conclusion to the subject of Web indexing. While we can answer some questions about Web indexing, more always arise. We already know that indexes on the Web can be an effective method of information retrieval. Indexers, with their ability to analyze information are prime candidates for creating online access tools. We must not allow fear of technology or the unknown deter us.

The waters of the Web are still choppy and the sea of information is dark, deep, and full of uncertainty. But what a voyage it will be!

REFERENCES

Merriam Webster's Collegiate Dictionary, Tenth Edition. Springfield, MA: Merriam Webster, 1993.

Wheatley, Henry Benjamin, *How to Make an Index.* London: Elliot Stock, 1902.

RESOURCES

Indexing Special Interest Group (SIG)

To meet others interested and involved in the field of Web indexing, contact ASI's Web Indexing Special Interest Group (SIG). See http://www.asindexing. org/sigs.htm for more information. The goals of the Web Indexing SIG are to promote the benefits of Web indexing; develop a Web site as a resource for indexers interested in Web indexing; and share ideas by having online forums to discuss tools, procedures, and marketing methods for Web indexing. For more information, contact: Kevin A. Broccoli, brocindx@catskill.net or (914) 985-9465, or Gerry Van Ravenswaay, gvrindex@xsite.net.

Web Indexing Tools

HTML Indexer, http://www.html-indexer.and http://www.brown-inc.com. David M. Brown's automated HTML indexing tool generates a formatted back of the book–style index. It's an HTML file that contains an alphabetized list of links to the files you include in your index project, to the named anchors within those files, and to any external URLs you choose to include in the project.

HTML/Prep, http://www.levtechinc.com/htmlprep.htm. This utility, used in conjunction with indexing software, such as Cindex or Macrex, allows you to prepare an index to Web sites and pages formatted as an HTML document.

HTML Help Workshop, http://www.microsoft.com/workshop/c-frame.htm#/workshop/ author/htmlhelp/default.asp. Microsoft's Site Builder Network home page. Workshops, articles, and information about Internet technologies, including reference material and in-depth articles on all aspects of Web site design and development.

WebWacker, http://www.bluesquirrel.com/products/whacker/whacker.html.This software allows you to download whole Web sites, including text, graphics, and HTML links, allowing you the luxury of examining at your leisure the construction of sites you admire.

Online Articles Related to Web Indexing

Broccoli, Kevin. "Indexes—an Old Tool for a New Medium" November 1998. http:// www. contentious.com/articles/1-8/guest1-8c.html. An in-depth examination of the process of Web site indexing.

Internet World. "Getting There, or Not: Why Search Is So Ineffective" February 1998.

http://www.internetworld.com/print/1998/02/23/news/19980223-search.html. A short article examining some of the problems associated with Web searches.

Rosenfeld, Lou. "Organizing Your Site from A to Z" October 1997. http://webreview. com/wr/pub/97/10/03/arch/index.html. An in-depth discussion of the development of a Web site index using the Adobe site as an example.

"Window on Web Indexing," a regular column in the Tennessee Regional Group of ASI's newsletter, *TennWords* http://members.aol.com/tennwords/home2.html. For more information, see also Broccoli Information Management, http://www.bim.net.

Chapter 5

Ripping Out the Pages

Seth Maislin © 1999

When the Web was invented, it was touted as a novel nonlinear medium for the written word. No longer would we be constrained by linear presentations! Hyperlinks would allow us to jump haphazardly from page to page, chapter to chapter, idea to idea! Texts would no longer need to run from beginning to end!

This is misleading. A printed book is also multidimensional and potentially nonlinear. We can open it to any page, from any other page, for any reason. We can open several books at once. In fact, what makes a book special is its combination of linear structure (the order of the words) and nonlinear physicality (the bound papers). This linear/nonlinear duality is enhanced further by the index, which maps linearly sequenced pages in a nonlinear, informationally ordered structure (architecture).

In truth, the online environment is crippled by an *absence* of linear structure. Imagine selecting a hard cover book, tearing off the covers, ripping pages into small pieces, and throwing them in a box. That box is like a computer file system, and the paper scraps are Web documents. Only one scrap can be retrieved from the box at a time, and it must be replaced before another can be accessed. Page numbers are meaningless. Global context is destroyed. And without page numbers or context, what happens to the index?

A NEW GENERATION OF INDEX

The fastest way to destroy an index is to destroy its page numbers, and sure enough, the World Wide Web doesn't have page numbers. Even more, embedded indexing techniques don't require the indexer's awareness of page numbers.

As an example of the scope of this dilemma, consider a single entry from a hypothetical back-of-the-book index:

Telegraph communications, 12, 44-56, 209

There is a lot of information here. We know that the bulk of information about telegraph communications starts on page 44. We can assume that page 12 provides an introductory comment. We can also assume that the entry for page 209 means a casual mention, since it comes so completely isolated from the other page numbers. If the book had 215 pages, we might accurately guess that the last entry comprises either a glossary item or a line in an appendix table.

Online, the entry might look a lot like this:

Telegraph communications, •, •, •

We no longer know which entry is the most important. We no longer understand how these documents fit into the entire collection of documents. We do not know the lengths of the documents themselves. We cannot even determine the order of the entries. Are they listed by importance, alphabetically by filename, or chronologically?

The loss of page numbers and of global context presents a fundamental handicap to writing a good index. Even the best indexing programs cannot work around these obstacles, since they are side-effects of the essential nature of online presentations. It is the indexer's responsibility to make accommodations for the environment.

There are other dilemmas as well, most of them related to layout. The designers of most authoring software have paid little attention to the need for indexes or to the indexing process. This is understandable because these applications are written for word processing, revision tracking, file conversion, or page layout. Indexing capabilities often are added as fancy enhancements. Even the applications that allow indexing have numerous shortcomings. Some don't allow for sub-subentries, cross-references, or special types of references. Most don't allow for locator-specific formatting. Many demonstrate inefficiencies in sorting index entries. Worst of all, HTML does not naturally allow for indentation.

Once we recognize the seriousness of the flaws inherent in online indexing, we know our challenges. We need to consciously and forcefully integrate context (and linearity) into our indexes. More specifically, we need to:

• Measure and rate index entries for importance or relevance.

• Understand the author's role in index quality.

• Clarify and communicate relationships among entries.

• Develop a visual architecture to demonstrate context, instead of concealing it.

• Take advantage of online technologies, such as interactivity.

The following sections examine ways of accomplishing these goals and overcoming the online environment challenges. Remember that every situation is different, and that different indexes serve different types of audiences. What works for one set of documents may not work for another. The index to an emergency-room reference needs to allow medical staff rapid access to very specific information, whereas corporate researchers might prefer dense, comprehensive lists of related information. Indexers must always recognize and respect the needs of users, and exercise this knowledge toward creating the best product possible.

RATING INDEX ENTRIES FOR IMPORTANCE OR RELEVANCE

Online, without a linear sequence to guide us, there is no intrinsic way of presenting information ranges. Furthermore, thanks to "document chunking" (breaking documents into small, more self-contained units), large quantities of information are generally split up. At first glance, all web pages may look like scraps of paper in a box.

Fortunately, text comes cheap in most online environments. Just as books have relatively verbose headers and footers, indexers can write locator text that explicitly communicates context. Interestingly, this is often taken for granted by authors and indexers alike, who tend to grab the nearest text, section title, or heading to provide the locator. Locator text should not be determined lightly. This is the indexer's only opportunity to provide context.

To demonstrate the possibilities, let's invent a baseline index for an online environment. Instead of page numbers, we'll use hyperlinks (represented here by underscoring) to the nearest section titles. Our index might look like this:

Telegraph communications

Dots and dashes

Electricity and its uses

History of early distance communication

The telegraph wire

These headings are rather descriptive. By reading through the choices (listed in alphabetical order, which is as arbitrary as it gets), we can confidently guess what these sections contain. Unfortunately, not all authors are as understanding of the user's needs. We might have an index like this:

Operator, I'd Like to Send a Message

Beep Beep Beep!

The Power of a Hot Wire

From Shouting to Carrier Pigeon

Hardware

To add to the confusion, you'll note that I did not re-alphabetize.

Authors need to keep section titles clear, though not necessarily short. Exactitude and wit can be combined, as in "Beep Beep Beep! The Language of Telegraphy" and "Distance Communication: From Shouting to Carrier Pigeon." Although some usability studies show that links containing six to ten words are the most effective, those studies looked at text headings, not indexes. Given that 90% of an index is comprised of links, the best way to improve usability is to avoid ambiguity. Even one-word locators like "Hardware" and "Electricity" are unambiguous to most of us.

Back-of-the-book indexes use numbered locators instead of text labels, as well as visual techniques that make the page numbers more meaningful. Boldface sometimes identifies locators that point to definitions, or italics are used for entries to illustrations. Additional visual cues can be added to online indexes. Color is readily available, and entries can be presented in enhanced font styles. Entries that are more important than others can be presented with larger lettering. Links to definitions or some other important body of text can be colored red. There are limits, of course. If you decide to use four different colors, two fonts, two font sizes, and four font styles, you will be creating a visual zoo that no one will want to visit. Visual enhancements such as fonts and colors should be used sparingly and only for clear, well-defined purposes.

A back-of-the-book technique similar to typography is to use text notations, such as the letters *i* for illustrations, *m* for maps, *f* for text in footnotes, and so on. This is easy to mimic online by putting an appropriate, unambiguous classification in parentheses after the link, such as, "From Shouting to Carrier Pigeon" (illus).

Sorting is another important tool. Alphabetizing is a randomizing process, so why not choose a sort order that makes more sense to the user? Possible sorting schemes include *chronology* (what comes first in time), *importance* (what is most valuable), *complexity* (what should be understood first), *application* (what comes first in the process), and *page order* (for print books converted to online documents). In addition, when there are many subentries, multiple sorting schemes can be used simultaneously. For example, the most important entries can come first, followed by a horizontal line or white space, followed by less important, page-number-ordered entries. In books, some indexers move entries for definitions or basic explanations to the tops of lists. Of course, most sorting schemes other than alphabetical are unfamiliar, so you need to provide an accessible explanation of the sorting scheme. Again, the more complicated the scheme, the faster readers get frustrated.

In addition to classifying and sorting, the web indexer can rate entries. You can, for example, display in boldface type any entry that meets a predefined threshold of importance. This is a binary rating system, in that the entry is either bold or not bold. Binary rating systems work poorly with subjective thresholds like "importance" or "relevance," because the reader usually does not understand the threshold. Continuous rating systems, such as type size (bigger equals more important) or color (red is more important than pink, for example), present another dilemma: ugliness. An index with a cornucopia of line sizes or colors looks unprofessional. In fact, the only real advantage to the binary and continuous rating systems is that they are both easy to implement.

A discrete rating system with three to five levels is better, similar to how movies are rated in the newspapers. The most intuitive of these is the "asterisk rating system," where each additional "star" represents slightly greater importance or relevance. The stars can be added to the beginnings or ends of the locators. Although this method can make an index look sloppy, no explanation is needed:

Telegraph communications ****

Dots and dashes

Electricity and its uses

History of early distance communication

The telegraph wire **

Another useful rating method involves tacking words or notations to entries, such as chapter titles or numbers, section titles, and other classifiers. This approach is useful when translating from hard copy. Notice in the following example that there are no special typography requirements, and that the notations are unambiguous.

Telegraph communications (Chap 5)

Dots and dashes (App C; table)

Electricity and its uses (Preface)

History of early distance communication (Chap 1)

History of early distance communication (Chap 1; illus)

The telegraph wire (Chap 5 Sect 1)

Of course, if there is no hard copy to refer to, "Chapter 5" becomes meaningless. Increasingly, online documentation is created without a hard copy version in mind, so more appropriate qualifiers need to be chosen. The qualifiers can be placed at the beginnings or ends of locators. Here are two examples, sorted by importance.

Telegraph communications (everything you ever wanted to know about the telegraph)

Electricity and its uses (introduction)

History of early distance communication (introduction)

History of early distance communication (poster-sized timeline, great for classrooms)

The telegraph wire (equipment and hardware)

Dots and dashes (table of telegraph codes)

Telegraph communications: Operator, I'd Like to Place a Call

Electricity introduction: The Power of a Hot Wire

Communications introduction: From Shouting to Carrier Pigeon

Communications timeline, poster-size: From Shouting to Carrier Pigeon

Telegraphy equipment: Hardware

Dot-dash telegraph codes, table: Beep Beep Beep!

THE AUTHOR'S ROLE IN WRITING A GOOD INDEX

As we have seen, the author's choice of section titles can provide some interesting challenges for the indexer. If the indexer is working with tools that disallow qualifiers or editing the locator text, bad section titles can destroy the index's value entirely. If you write web documents, consider these guidelines. If you are working with a web page author, pass along this advice to help make your indexing job easier:

Use uniform page sizes. Selecting one index entry over another should not be a game of chance, particularly because most hyperlinks look the same. Links at the bottoms of pages to other pages—sections of related topics, or even "continued lines"—can provide continuity without sacrificing a comfortable sense of uniformity. Shorter pages provide flow throughout the documentation, since the reader is constantly moving from one page to the next. Monitor space is limited, so shorter pages make for simpler reading and less scrolling. Finally, given the expectations of many online readers, compact units of information are likely to be appreciated.

Provide lists of related topics and references. Navigating an online index can be difficult, but having to navigate between the index and the content pages is especially annoying. Give the reader an "out" by writing explicit topical paths for readers to follow. Your lists of related topics demonstrate your interest in providing a good index.

Compartmentalize your ideas. The ability to write single pages about single topics is a feature of online environments, because page length is controlled by your imagination. Take advantage of the environment by chunking sensibly, thus eliminating the index's need for the absent "page range" concept.

Be somewhat redundant. Without context, readers no longer know what they can expect. And if readers can't find it, they will assume it does not exist. By writing everything more than once in different formats, a reader is given multiple entry points to the same ideas.

Develop a clear information hierarchy. Although knowledge does not often fit neatly into titled categories, web users look for modular information "packages" anyway. Write related topics lists to guide users from one package to the next, and use redundancy to fill information gaps instead of directing users into other packages. If your pages are comprehensive, you still may find that certain pages fit into multiple categories.

Use design elements for categorization. Thumbnail images in book margins can identify important concepts, textual elements, and certain types of activities. On the Web, colors, background patterns, and sound are available alternatives for providing contextual clues to the reader, if used conservatively. Where a commercial Web site might use certain design elements to illustrate a cohesive corporate identity, so can you use graphic design to clarify purpose, content types, content age, geographical relevance, and audience.

COMMUNICATING RELATIONSHIPS AMONG ENTRIES

Cross-references are more complicated online, but they are as essential as in stand-alone indexes. Many tools for embedding indexing do not offer complete freedom when it comes to writing or displaying cross-references. Quantities of online information can grow very large or change daily. Documents can move from one URL to another, resulting in outdated links. Online documentation is not even limited to a single Internet site. Hyperlinks can extend beyond the author's scope by pointing to documentation written by somebody else, in a different language, in a different context. Still, even with all these complications, cross-references are an important part of communicating the relationships between index entries. Here are some simple tips:

- Navigating online indexes can be difficult because of their length, so use *See* cross-references carefully. If two main-level terms are effectively identical, post the index information at both locations to help readers avoid unnecessary navigation.

- *See* references are a great technique to manage users' word choices. Asking the user to follow one more hyperlink can help you educate the users toward your preferred vocabulary set. This becomes even more important if the index is enhanced by a search engine, because search engines do not handle synonyms or related terminology.

- Present *See also* cross-references as early as possible, such as at the top of a subentry list (instead of at the bottom). This way users can more quickly understand the document structure.

- Use *See also* cross-references to point to other locations within the index, appropriate reference lists within the document, transitory web pages, and web sites outside the documentation (e.g., "*See also* information provided at various <u>Online Shopping Centers for Telegraphy Accessories</u>").

- In a hyperlinked index, use circular *See also* references so that readers can retrace their steps.

- "Related Topics" paragraphs in the documentation itself not only work similarly to *See also* cross-references, but they also provide clues that can help the person writing the index.

There is an interesting online alternative to multiple cross-references: multiple indexes. This is the approach used by web page designers to make a site's home page comprehensive without overloading it with text. For example, if there were enough information about Telegraphy in our hypothetical book, we could create a specialized Telegraphy Index and create links to it from the main index. This possibility will be discussed below in greater detail.

Finally, the most obvious technique for demonstrating relationships between index entries is usually absent from most online indexes: multiple hyperlinks for a single locator. For example, as we've seen, the back-of-the-book entry "Telegraph communications, 12, 44-56, 209" would usually be presented using the multilined locator approach shown above. Fortunately, there are other options.

Simple numbers are sufficient when images are presented: "Pictures of the White House, U.S.: <u>1</u>, <u>2</u>, <u>3</u>, <u>4</u>." The assumption here is that the images are of equal value.

In addition, if there are locators to both text and special text elements, the links can be labeled as such: "From Shouting to Carrier Pigeon: text; illus."

Chronological values are often sufficient for links, either because they have meaning within the document, or because they represent the date or time that the information was added to the index: "Human embryo, stages of: <u>Day 1</u>, <u>Day 2</u>, <u>Day 5</u>, <u>Day 15</u>, <u>Day 30</u>, ..." If subentries are short, they themselves can be combined on a single line: "Summer tourism activities: <u>June</u>, <u>July</u>, <u>August</u>."

In most cases, however, the link text needs to be longer than one or two words, or else there are so many links that long strings of them are hard to read. The first option is to break them up into smaller, subentry-like groups. This type of breakdown also lends itself to creating multiple indexes:

> Computer privacy laws, by state
>
> <u>Alabama</u> | <u>Alaska</u> | <u>Arizona</u> | <u>Arkansas</u>
>
> <u>California</u> | <u>Colorado</u> | <u>Connecticut</u>
>
> <u>Delaware</u> | <u>District of Columbia</u>

> Manager contact information, by department
> Human Resources: <u>Beverly White</u> | <u>Violet Rogelman</u>
> Personnel (Hiring): <u>Patrick Beige</u>
> Technical Support: <u>Judith "Blue" Screen</u> | <u>Turq Woise</u> | <u>Wayne Bow</u>

Mostly, however, we are simply forced to use much longer locators, such as section titles. If locators are long enough, they do deserve their own lines.

The following layout is my personal favorite for an HTML index. It sorts either alphabetically or by importance, depending on context. It allows enough room to add qualifiers such as those discussed above. Most subentries get their own line, but lists of cross-references are combined horizontally, with semicolons between them. Note that this layout is reproducible using standard HTML definition lists:

> Communications technologies
> > *See also* <u>Computers</u>; <u>Electronic mail</u>; <u>Language acquisition</u>; <u>Spoken languages</u>; <u>Written languages</u>
> > <u>History of early distance communication</u> (introduction)
> > <u>Accessibility software for computer users</u>
>
> Electricity for communications
> > <u>Electricity and its uses</u> (introduction)
> > <u>Invention of the telephone</u>
> > <u>History of early distance communication</u> (illustrated timeline, poster-size)
> > <u>Discovering electricity at home</u> (hands-on activities for kids)
>
> Telegraphy
> > <u>Telegraph communications</u>
> > Codes, telegraphic: <u>Dots and dashes</u>
> > Hardware and equipment: <u>The telegraph wire</u>

Telephones and faxes: *See* <u>Fax communications</u>; <u>Telephony</u>

This design uses almost all of the techniques mentioned in this section, and it is visually complicated. However, in most circumstances the underscoring would be replaced with link colors, and the unlinked text would stand out clearly.

Whatever design is chosen, it should allow enough horizontal space for qualified links, enough vertical space for entries and subentries, a visible white space between topics and subtopics, clear and unambiguous lists of cross-references, and no conceptually overlapping subentries.

DEVELOPING A VISUAL ARCHITECTURE AND NAVIGATION SYSTEM

Design is a serious impediment when presenting online indexes. HTML is a miserable tool for writing an index. In fact, it is not uncommon for an author or indexer to spend more time designing and editing the format than actually writing the index or adding context to the locators. Yet beyond all that, when the index is indented well and written consistently, a whole new set of difficulties arises: the index is a document in itself. All the concerns of authors suddenly become concerns for the indexers, too.

Consider the example at the end of the previous section. Imagine that the entry "Communications technologies" is simply one of many on a page containing 200 lines of index. Imagine scrolling down that page until the entry "Communications technologies" is the second-highest visible line on the page, such that there is a single index entry or link above it. That line might be:

<u>List of, by state</u> (table)

Without being able to see the main entry a few lines higher, this line of the index is useless. Readers easily lose track of their search in extremely long lists of subentries. Back-of-the-book indexes use "continued" lines when a list of subentries runs across two pages, but online indexes cannot do this without more complicated programming. Fortunately, we have other options. One involves using HTML frames, with highest-level index entries in one frame and selected subentries in another frame. If the index is extremely long and complicated, a better option uses multiple indexes.

The first question is, how many separate pages should your index have? Should you use one giant page, or should you break your index into as many as 26 pages, one for each letter of the alphabet? The main challenge when writing many index pages is to develop a good navigation system. Since the user can't flip pages, it is up to you to create paths that readers can use to get around your index. The advantage to having one giant page is that a reader can scan the index without trouble, reading entirely through it without interruption. The disadvantage is that a single web page with thousands of lines can be daunting.

Breaking a long index into pages by letter is a common option. At the top of each page is a navigation bar of letters, with each letter linked to one of the index pages:

52

<u>A</u> I <u>B</u> I <u>C</u> I <u>D</u> I <u>E</u> I <u>F</u> I <u>G</u> I <u>H</u> I <u>I</u> I <u>J</u> I <u>K</u> I <u>L</u> I <u>M</u> I <u>N</u> I <u>O</u> I <u>P</u> I <u>R</u> I <u>S</u> I <u>T</u> I <u>U</u> I <u>V</u> I <u>W</u> I <u>Y</u>

Where are Q, X, and Z? Occasionally index navigation bars omit letters if no words in the index start with them, yet it looks awkward without them. English-language users are so familiar with the 26-letter alphabet that they may be confused by this. Leaving letters out of navigation bars is not recommended. Instead, include them without links. Not only is it less jarring, but it permits the index to grow and accommodate any new terms.

Of course, letters can be grouped together or divided further. Consistency is key.

<u>A to D</u> I <u>E to H</u> I <u>I to L</u> I <u>M to P</u> I <u>Q to T</u> I <u>U to Z</u>

<u>Aa–Am</u> I <u>An–Az</u> I <u>Ba–Bz</u> I ... I <u>Sa–Sh</u> I <u>Si–Sn</u> I <u>So–Sz</u> I ... I <u>Xa–Xy</u> I <u>Ya–Yz</u> I <u>Za–Zy</u>

As for scrolling from one letter group to the next, a link can be placed at the bottom of each page, pointing to the next page. In addition, the navigation bar could be repeated, so that a reader who wants to jump ahead doesn't need to scroll back to the top of the page. Alternatively, the navigation bar (along with Next and Previous buttons) could be placed in a frame that doesn't scroll, at the top, bottom, or side.

Also important are navigation tools used to move around among individual index tags, such as cross-references. For example, one idea is to present all *See also*–style cross-references circularly, so that a user can follow "related topics connections" in either direction. Another suggestion is to ensure that cross-reference hyperlinks point to the nearest main entry, not to the subentries. Consider the following example:

Electricity, communication-related. *See* <u>Communications technologies,</u> <u>Electricity for communications</u>

If the hyperlink points to the index line "Electricity for communications," the main heading ("Communications technologies") would be lost since it would appear too high to fit in the window. Also lost are important cross-references. The reader would have to scroll up to identify the context, an unnecessary added step.

- - - - top of display - - - -

Electricity for communications

    <u>Electricity and its uses</u> (introduction)
    <u>Invention of the telephone</u>
    <u>History of early distance communication</u> (illustrated timeline, poster-size)
    <u>Discovering electricity at home</u> (hands-on activities for kids) . . . .

Without the context, readers no longer know where they are in the index. Hyperlinks to points inside the index should always point to the highest level possible. In HTML, then, the target of the *href* attribute should lead the reader to "Communications technologies," but the text within the <A> tags should contain the subentry text, "Communications technologies, Electricity for communications." Also capitalize the first letter of the subentry text within the link, because punctuation is a common feature of web-based section titles and headings.

Not surprisingly, web addresses (such as URLs) can aid navigation as well. Naming your files and anchors intuitively and unambiguously can give the reader even more clues about hyperlinks. Remember that each page's web address appears at the top of the browser, and that selected hyperlink addresses can be made visible in the browser status bar. Take advantage of these features by naming documents well. Although some systems require filenames to be no longer than eight characters, content naming is still better than number-based naming in most situations. Filenames like *telegrap.htm* and *electric.htm* are good content labels, as opposed to *chapter5.htm*. Even worse are computer-generated filenames that defy human interpretation, like *elpg5-3f.htm*.

One of the best frameworks for presenting an index is linking together multiple indexes. Because indexes can grow very long, and because vertical scrolling has the potential to hide context, there are obvious advantages to "chunking" the index, in the same way that authors are urged to write in discrete units. Among the many possible ways of providing multiple indexes are these four:

Alphabet-based subindexes. If an index gets too long, split it up. Dividing up an index by letters of the alphabet, for example, is an easy way to avoid writing an unmanageably large index.

Chronologically based subindexes. Activity lists might use seasons, months, or days of the week as intuitive reader-friendly divisions. Automobile specification data might be divided up by model year. If information lends itself to a chronological breakdown, consider writing different indexes for different time units.

Subject-based subindexes. If your documentation lends itself to discrete topics, then a natural breakdown exists. Consider writing one index for each subject. For example, a user manual about electronic mail could provide one index for each email application, since users may be interested only in software they use.

Audience-oriented subindexes. Different readers have different needs. You can cater to those needs by providing customized indexes. Educational texts provide different sets of information for teachers and students, and a more inclusive teacher index is an appropriate tool. Similarly, if you know the operating system or platform of your user (and with JavaScript this is easy to determine), you can provide indexes to them without including any distracting system- or platform-specific hyperlinks. This works especially well if some content is unavailable to certain users, since a separate and more comprehensive index can be password protected.

The most effective way to use multiple indexes is to create a master index from which the subindexes are accessible. The master index would then contain only the highest-level entries necessary to itemize the subindexes. At an extreme, subindexing looks a lot like information architecture and web design:

Global Index	Teacher Pages	Teacher Resources Online
Student Pages	Lesson Planner	Libraries Online
Parent Information	Grading Forms	Downloadable Activities
Teacher Pages→	Online Resources→	Workbook Solutions

The goals of subindexing are identical to those of indexing in general, to get the reader to all desired information as fast as possible. As a result, the extra steps involved in navigating through subindexes may prove more of a hindrance rather than a help. Multiple indexes should be used only when they contain enough information to deserve their own page.

You might also consider writing indexes that present the same information sorted differently, just as a list of books can be listed by title, author name, subject, year of publication, and so on. In fact, by presenting the same information in several differently sorted indexes, you can preclude the need for search engine technology. In that case you are considering not the background of your users, but rather their needs. A book about automobiles, for example, could be enhanced by including indexes for model names and numbers, manufacturer names, and years.

USING ONLINE TECHNOLOGIES

The Web is not simply "a better book," but it does present more opportunities than paper can. For example, search engines do not work without computers. Color, sound, and animation are available inexpensively. Web documentation can be updated moment by moment. Distribution is cheap.

When it comes to indexing, however, few of these features have serious advantages. Sound and color often distract more than they enhance. And search engines have become an indexer's nightmare. The tendency to "click first and ask questions later" has helped text searches grow so commonplace that most users bypass indexes in favor of a perceived increase in speed. Because search engines are so easy to build, and because there are so few online indexes (and even fewer of quality), indexes get ignored. But indexes offer a level of intelligence and thought that search engines will never reproduce. By choosing a search engine over an index, the user is choosing the "dumb" option.

Search engines will never be replaced by indexes either. If authors decide to use both search engines and indexes, here's some sound advice: Put the index first, and force users to navigate past the index to get to the search interface. You can even imply that the search engine is an inferior option: "If you can't find what you're looking for in the index, try our search engine page." Search engines are nightmarish only in their influence over users looking for the quick answer.

Text searches have one amazing power, however. When a user knows precisely what he wants, down to the character, a search engine has a perfect record in locating that item. Search engines perform beautifully in locating all instances of (correctly spelled) proper nouns, for example. Although many commercial search engines are enhanced by ratings algorithms, search engines usually fail to accurately attribute importance to various results. An index, on the other hand, by implementing the simple tradition of indenting subtopics, visually illustrates levels of importance and relevance. This interpretative process is what makes the index intelligent, and is among the reasons why good indexes will never be created by machine.

Web documents offer indexers one serious technological advantage over books: interactivity. Online documentation can be highly dynamic. JavaScript rollovers are one straightforward example. When a user moves the cursor over a particular object within a web document, such as a hyperlink or an image, JavaScript code can execute color changes, image switching, and pop-up text. In this way users can interact directly with the document.

Similarly, pop-up text can be very useful in displaying link descriptors such as those described above. Instead of maintaining a long index, JavaScript can be used to "relocate" text to a central location. For example, consider these two indexes:

Telegraph communications	Telegraph communications (Chap 5)
Dots and dashes	Dots and dashes (App C; table)
Electricity and its uses	Electricity and its uses (Preface)
History of early distance communication	History of early distance communication (Chap 1)
The telegraph wire	The telegraph wire (Chap 5 Sect 1)

The annotated index on the right contains more information, but visually the index requires more horizontal space, and the parenthetical statements are visually distracting. With JavaScript, the annotations could appear in a separate place on the display, in either the browser's status bar or in a specially designed frame. Thus the final index would appear like the example on the left, yet the annotations would be available for those interested in reading them.

By creating a much larger frame dedicated to pop-up information, annotations of much greater length become possible. An interesting application of this is an index of main entries in which rollovers portray subentry information in a separate frame. This system works best when there are different main entries but similar subentries, or when the subentries are all similar in purpose or style. Consider a customer service manual at a financial institution, in which representatives are expected to perform similar tasks when a customer opens a new account. The main index would list the account types, and the frames index would list the tasks available to customer service:

Account Management	Stock Account Options
Bonds	Opening a new account
IRAs and retirement plans	Retrieving account balance
Mutual funds	Redistributing funds to different
Stocks➔	Accounts address, name, and status
	Changes
	Closing the account

It is worth recognizing that color is already used to mark links that have been followed. Graphical web browsers today change the color of links when those links have been visited. This coloring system works well with indexing because good indexes will allow multiple entry points for the same documentation; selecting one path will mark all other paths to the same destination as having been selected. Unfortunately, this can also be misleading, because some authors limit the possible hyperlink targets to headings or the tops of documents. Longer sections, therefore, will be labeled as "visited" even if the user investigated only a small portion of the text. This is another argument in favor of writing shorter sections and being slightly redundant in presentation.

Another online technology is the use of downloads. Depending on the content and the audience, users may download documentation from the Internet so that they can refer to it later without reconnecting. However, because online indexes are dependent on successful hyperlinks, moving a file from one platform to another (such as from online to a desktop computer) can seriously affect the index's functionality. Take this into consideration when designing the index. Any downloads should include either the entire index or no index at all. Provide a different version of the index specifically for download. Use relative web addresses whenever possible. Ultimately, the indexer's goal must be to preserve the integrity of the links. Many utilities specifically designed to check hyperlinks are available over the Internet at no cost. Be sure to choose a utility that checks links from one page to another as well as links within the same page.

CONCLUSION

Anything that you can do in a book, you can do online. But the online environment is nothing like a book in its structure and traditions. More than 50 years after the invention of the back-of-the-book index, indexers still debated if alphabetizing were the best approach. (See Wheatley, Henry Benjamin, *How to Make an Index* (London: Elliot Stock, 1902).) These arguments continue today regarding online indexes, as demonstrated by the multitude of online lists that are organized chronologically, geographically, and even metaphorically. Further, the very definition of "online indexing" is in flux. The theory and practice of online indexing overlap several other fields of study, including design, information architecture, programming, and cognitive science.

Now is not the time to develop standards and traditions. Our goal is to experiment, with as full an understanding of this new medium as possible, by seeking out and studying examples of indexes. We should also observe how indexes are used and request feedback from users. We should remain open to new and intriguing possibilities, and then publicly share these ideas.

REFERENCES

Cunningham, Steve and Jason Rosebush. *Electronic Publishing on CD-ROM*. Sebastopol, CA: O'Reilly & Associates, 1996.

Killelea, Patrick. *Web Performance Tuning*, Sebastopol. CA: O'Reilly & Associates, 1998, Chapter 14.

McCloud, Scott. *Understanding Comics: The Invisible Art. New York*: HarperCollins, 1994.

Rosenfeld, Louis and Peter Morville. *Information Architecture for the World Wide Web*. Sebastopol, CA: O'Reilly & Associates, 1998.

Chapter 6

Plunging In:
Creating a Web Site Index for an
Online Newsletter

Marilyn J. Rowland

Creating an online index for a Web site is not a job for the timid. Those contemplating this form of Web indexing should already be accomplished indexers and should have strong experience in Web page creation. Knowledge of HTML is essential. In fact, depending on the nature of a Web indexing job, you may find that it requires more HTML knowledge than indexing skill.

Like embedded indexing, Web site indexing is far more work than traditional indexing: the choice of terms is constrained, and the indexing process itself is slower and more challenging. Entries must be carefully chosen because the editing process can be tedious and time-consuming, sometimes more time-consuming than making the original entries. Hypertext links and anchors must be added, and the index itself must be tested to make sure that links work as intended. Adequate compensation for your project is imperative.

Web indexing does have its rewards, though, especially for indexers who are intrigued by the Web and Web page design, for those who like a challenge, and, of course, for those who like to have their work online for all the world to see.

This article provides a look at the process of creating a Web index for an online newsletter. It is also applicable to other forms of Web site indexing, and should give the beginning Web site indexer an idea of what to expect on that first job.

DIVERSITY OF WEB SITE INDEXING

There are probably as many forms of site-based Web indexing as there are Web sites and clients. How you go about creating a Web index may depend on:

59

- What type of a site you are indexing. For example, an online publication, an information-packed site housing the results of numerous research reports on a wide range of topics; a small general information site on a specific topic; or a dynamic site with rapidly changing content.
- Whether you have created the Web site or have any involvement in its administration, or whether you are hired as part of a team of webmasters specifically for the job of Web indexing.
- Whether it's a one-time indexing project, perhaps with minor updating as the site is modified or whether a site that is substantially modified on a regular basis (for instance, an online newsletter), or a site that changes daily.
- Whether the index is intended as a simple navigation aid, or a detailed research aid, and whether other tools, such as menus and search tools are also provided on the site.

A SPECIFIC EXAMPLE: INDEXING AN ONLINE NEWSLETTER

Rather than attempt to cover every possibility you might encounter, I will discuss my experiences with a specific type of Web index: an extensive index for an online newsletter, *Case-in-Point*, published by Cross World Network for Acxiom Corporation, a database services provider. *Case-in-Point* is a bimonthly (soon-to-be-quarterly) newsletter concerning the use and management of marketing information (e.g., customer and prospect data) and data-driven strategies. The newsletter is circulated in print to senior marketing executives and CIOs (chief information officers) and is available at no charge on the Web. The index helps users find what they need in Acxiom's extensive library of print and online materials. In January 1999 Acxiom had published over 22 issues, 49 stand-alone case studies, and 34 in-depth reports. All are online and indexed. The index is also useful for those who read the print newsletter. Because it is expensive to keep a printed index up to date and useful for readers, *Case-in-Point* refers its print readers to the online index.

The *Case-in-Point* index site already included three years of online newsletters, reports and case studies by the time I was hired at the beginning of year four. By that time, the index design and the indexing process had been well-established. Now, in year five, it is a very large Web index with over 4,000 entries. There are now several sub-indexes to help readers find topics and browse the index more readily. At the end of each article, case study, and report is a link to a keywords page that allows the reader to see what keywords (index terms) were chosen for each article. Readers can follow keywords of interest back to index itself to find other related articles. This feature makes the index particularly useful for readers interested in researching a particular topic.

There has been some discussion of dropping the index in favor of the existing site search engine, or an upgraded version of it, but there are those, myself included, who believe that a browsable index offers certain advantages over a site search tool, particularly in a constantly changing and terminology-filled field like data management. An index helps the user find the exact term she is looking for, whereas a search engine may provide a hodge-podge of near-misses. An index gives the user a sense of the contents of the site that he cannot get from typing a word or phrase into a fill-in form. An index provides *See* and *See also* references, which further help the user define her topic. Still, an index is slower than a search engine tool, and it may not meet the needs of those who require instant gratification. A long and complex index, like the one for *Case-in-Point*, may be slow to navigate. Perhaps the best solution is the one taken by Acxiom, offering readers both a search tool and an index, as well as other navigation tools such as menus, site maps, tables of contents.

Whether this is a "typical" Web indexing project is hard to say, but it does give those considering Web indexing a good idea of one approach to this type of work and the process involved.

WEB SITE INDEXING PROCESS

1. *Select the index terms.* The first step in the Web indexing process, as in most indexing jobs, is to pick the terms to be included in the index. Because I am adding terms to an existing online index, I am not free to choose index terms, but have to be sure that the new terms are consistent with those already in the index. This is similar to periodical indexing. I have to consult the existing index to determine whether the term is already in the index and how it is phrased, whether there are any spelling inconsistencies, whether the term currently has subentries or not, and whether the concept has a "See" reference in the current index and should be indexed under a different term.

   The existing index is huge, consisting of 22 long Web pages. The letter "D" page, containing many topics related to "Data," is over 20 feet in length when printed out. I open the index in my browser, offline, and navigate through it to check new terms against existing terms.

   Because the newsletter uses a specialized vocabulary, the client reviews the indexing terms article-by-article to be sure important terms are present and that they are referenced correctly. This review is important to the overall quality of the index, but it does create an additional step for me. Once I have selected the index terms, I must prepare an article-by-article list of terms for each of the dozen or so articles in each issue of the newsletter for client review before compiling the terms into a single index for the issue. I could start by creating a composite index of all the terms for a single issue, creating a better index product by identifying and resolving inconsistencies in terminology among articles, but then I would have to disaggregate the terms into separate articles for submission to the client. I am working on finding time-efficient ways to improve the indexing process.

2. *Client review of index terms.* I generally fax or email a list of terms to the client and she reviews for company style, appropriate terminology, accuracy, and consistency with the existing index, usually returning the list of terms with her suggestions in a couple of days. Sometimes we discuss her changes or suggestions and come up with alternate wording; sometimes we decide to change existing index entries to conform to new buzzwords or to reflect company name changes. In many ways, this early review by the client is helpful; it is somewhat like doing the editing and getting approval on the job in advance of entering the index terms. But this review does slow down and interrupt the flow of entering the terms, and it does not always resolve all inconsistencies. Preapproval of terms also creates more difficulty for me to change them later on when I am actually inserting the terms into the index and find that they don't fit the index exactly as planned.

3. *Consolidation of index terms.* I make whatever changes the client requests or that we have agreed upon. Then I type the index into my indexing program (CINDEX, Windows 95 version), creating a composite index for all the articles, reports, and case studies in that particular issue of the newsletter. Usually, at this point I see some glaring inconsistency that was not apparent in the earlier stage when terms were listed separately under each article. I fix these errors, occasionally querying the client.

Below is an example of the index product showing how "page numbers" are entered. Actual page numbers are irrelevant, of course; Web indexes include hypertext links to the page. In the *Case-in-Point* index, hypertext links are created on the name of the article in which the term appears. Article names are prefaced by a code indicating whether the article is a case study (CS), a report (R), or a newsletter article (N). The numbers indicate the volume and issue number. Thus, in the example below, N4.2 means a newsletter article in volume 4, issue 2. The article name thus becomes the "page number" in the index. If you click on the name of the article, you will move to the top of the page containing the article. (This index does not include anchors to take the reader to specific places within the articles, just to the top of the page. See below for more discussion on this. Note also that in this index, boldface indicates an Acxiom client.) Thus, if you are looking for an article on revenue growth, you have a choice of two articles. You can decide which article meets your needs by looking at the subentries and at the names of the articles in which these topics appear. To get to the article/report/case study, click on the article/report/case study name:

Revenue data
   CS: Bell Atlantic
Revenue growth
   data warehouses and

To create this structure in CINDEX, I can not put the "page numbers" (article names) in the page number field because CINDEX would put the article names in a single line, one after another, rather than place them as subentries, or sub-subentries, as above. Thus, I ignore the page number field in CINDEX and simply enter the article names as subentries or sub-subentries.

Once the terms are entered and edited as necessary, I create an RTF file of the index, open it in Word and save it as an HTML document.

4. *Creation of Interim Web page.* I open the HTML document in NetscapeComposer and edit it as necessary. I add hypertext links for all the article names, with Composer, using a copy-and-paste approach to minimize the actual number of times I have to create a link. This time-saving method has problems of its own though; I once copy-and-pasted an inaccurate link through half the index before I noticed the error.

I then open the existing index (the 22 separate Web pages) in another Netscape Composer window. I use Composer, a WYSIWYG HTML-authoring program, because it is easier for me to insert new terms into the existing index when I can clearly see the terms, uncluttered by HTML codes. I copy and paste each term from one Composer screen to the other, carrying the hypertext links from my initial Web index page to the existing index pages. I occasionally make errors in alphabetical order when I do this, causing me to reflect on the primitiveness of this method of doing things. I continue to find inconsistencies in terminology as I continue with the copy-and-paste routine, and I continue to correct them.

I use HTML definition lists to format the index. Definition lists have two parts: a term and a definition for that term. <DT> tags are used for the terms; <DD> tags are used for the definitions, and the entire list is enclosed in <DL> tags. In a Web index, <DT> tags can be used for the main entry, and <DD> tags can be used for the subentries. Omitting link tags in this example to avoid confusion, the HTML formatting for the first few lines of the above index segment looks like this:

```
<DL>
<DT>Revenue data</DT>
<DD>CS: <B>Bell Atlantic</B></DD>
<DT>Revenue growth</DT>
<DD>data warehouses and
<DL><DD> R4.2: "ROI Considerations for a Data Warehouse
Project</DD></DL>
<DD>stages of</DD>
<DL><DD>N4.2: "Data--The Fluid Asset</DD>
</DL>
</DL>
```

Note that closing </DT> and </DD> tags are not required. (*See* Chapter 11, "Putting Sample Indexes on Your Web Site" by Rachel Rice for more information on HTML coding for indexes.) I continue to use them because the original indexer used them, and I like consistency. For indexes with more than two levels, <DL> tags can be nested to create further indentations:

```
The code <DL>
<DT>main heading</DT>
<DD>subentry one</DD>
<DD>subentry two</DD>
<DL>
<DD>sub-subentry</DD>
</DL>
</DL>
```

will print as:

main heading
   subentry one
   subentry two
      sub-subentry

Netscape Composer uses another method (<DIV> tags) to create indented text, and these two methods are not always compatible, so I usually end up doing far more manual adjusting of HTML code than I would like to do, but the alternative, typing in all the codes by hand, is not appealing to me.

As noted above, the Acxiom index uses **boldface** to emphasize the names of their customers. I format these words as boldface in CINDEX, and the formatting survives the transition from CINDEX to Word to Composer.

5. *Keeping Track of Inconsistencies.* As I enter the terms, I usually find problems and inconsistencies with wording that did not show up during my first comparison of new terms with existing terms, or during the client review process. I make minor changes and query the client on any problems I can't resolve, such as similar, but not quite the same names for companies. For instance, I recently found the following entries in the index:

First Manhattan Consulting Group

First Manhattan Group

Manhattan Consulting Group

Suspecting they were variants of one company, but not knowing for sure, I queried the client. She confirmed that the company name for all three should be First Manhattan Consulting Group, and I made changes throughout.

In addition to making changes in the index, I have to track the changes and make sure they are all entered into my CINDEX file for the index. It is important that the CINDEX file reflects what is actually in the index because the CINDEX files for each issue are combined to produce a cumulative index. This cumulative index (though it does not include hypertext links) serves as the official record and can be used to make a print copy of the entire index. It is also useful in searching for and grouping concepts during index creation and editing, just as in traditional indexing.

Keeping track of the changes tends to be a bit tedious, and, invariably, I forget some of them. Occasionally, I compare the two files side-by-side, to make sure all important changes are transferred and that the CINDEX file is as accurate as possible.

6. *Adding anchors.* As mentioned above, the *Case-in-Point* index does not link to anchors in the newsletter pages. In other words, it does not direct the user to the actual point in a newsletter article where the subject is mentioned. It just takes users to the top of the page. When I took on this job, I suggested to the client that we add anchors. She suggested we wait and concentrate on bringing the index up-to-date. The index was about three issues behind the publication of the newsletter when I started. I am grateful for the client's caution, in terms of workload. Adding targets, though easy enough to do in HTML, is time-consuming and requires numerous judgment calls as to exact placement of the targets and how to treat extended passages (the online equivalent of page ranges) or separated references in the same article. Because the newsletter articles are relatively short (the equivalent of one to five print pages) and fairly specific in

nature, although the index link takes you only to the top of the article page, this is not a major inconvenience to most users.

The *Case-in-Point* index does, however, make substantial use of anchors in another way. I mark each main entry and some subentries with an anchor when I insert it into the index pages. This allows me to easily create *See* and *See also* references, and it supports the extensive system of keyword indexes, or, as I tend to think of them, "reverse" indexes.

The "reverse" indexes help the reader find articles related to the one he has just read. At the end of each article is a link to a "Keywords" list that displays the subject and company name index entries for each article. By clicking on a keyword, the user is returned to the index where he can find other articles that were indexed with the same keyword.

Thus, the anchors next to each index entry term are needed to allow the links to work in the keywords pages.

7. *Testing, modifying, and rechecking formatting.* At this point the main index is substantially complete, but I am only about halfway through the job. Now, I test the index by reviewing it carefully in my browser(s) to see how it will look online. I make changes as necessary. Then I check formatting again to make sure the index looks the way I want it to. Finally satisfied, I compress the 24 index files into one zip file, using WinZip for Windows 95, and email it off to the Acxiom Webmaster, who puts the index online.

Invariably, I find a formatting error a minute later. I correct the error, but don't resend the file right away—just in case I find a few more.

8. *Create keyword index pages for articles, reports, and case studies.* After I send off the main index pages, I turn my attention to creating keyword pages for the "reverse indexes." For this task, I return to my original list of keywords for each article, report, and case study, as modified by the indexing process. The articles and reports keywords pages each contains a list of keywords by article/report in chronological order. The case studies keyword page lists case studies in alphabetical order by name of company. All keywords pages have links that allow the user to return to the article she just read, go to a new article, or be transported to the index to see related articles.

This process is time-consuming, but not difficult, and eventually I have three more pages to send to the Webmaster. I zip them and email them off.

9. *Update the Companies, People, Products/Services, Organizations, Subjects indexes.* The Case-in-Point index is actually six indexes. In addition to the 24-page main index, there are also specialized long, one-page indexes listing companies, people, products and services, and main subjects. Now, I go back to my original list of index entries (as modified during the indexing process) and divide them into these five categories. I am working on a way to pre-identify each term by category to see if I can automate this part of the process somewhat. For now, though, this part of the job repeats items 4, 6, and 7, above, five more times.

10. *Send and re-send the index files.* Finally, I am finished. I zip the specialized index files and email them off to the Webmaster. I check the 24-page main index one more time, correcting any problems or inconsistencies I find, sometimes querying the client, even at this late point in the process. I zip any page files I have changed and send them off too.

11. *Update the CINDEX file.* Now, I update the CINDEX file for the current issue, based on various notes I have taken throughout the indexing process. I then copy the current index file into the cumulative index file. I check the resulting index briefly and save the file, both as an index file and as a text file. I open the text file in Word and print out the index. Finally, I overnight the printout of the index and a disk file of the index (which has to be zipped to fit on the disk) to the client. I'm now done, until the next issue.

CONCLUSION

On the whole, I thoroughly enjoy the process of Web indexing; I find it challenging and absorbing. It is, however, extraordinarily time-consuming and the occasional "unsolvable" HTML problem can be exasperating. There are many Web indexing tools on the market that promise to help the indexer/Web designer create indexes quickly and easily, but I have yet to find the one that meets the needs of this project. I am hopeful, though. The design of the index itself is evolving, and the capabilities of Web indexing programs are changing. It may not be long before the two meet and the process of indexing a large online periodical is simplified considerably.

For those interested in or involved in designing a large Web index, I offer some suggestions based on my experience with this project.

- Use subentries and sub-subentries to supply additional information, as in the Acxiom index, rather than providing blank, non-identifying links or a single link to the main entry. Users can get some sense of whether the subject is briefly mentioned or a main topic of the article by looking at the title of the article.

- A "reverse index" can be very helpful in guiding users to related Web pages. Another way to achieve this is through *See also* entries at the end of each article, as is usually done in interactive encyclopedias. Maintaining an up-to-date list of links at the end of each article or Web page would add considerable work to preparing the index, unless the process were automated in some fashion.

- A system of multiple indexes (subject, name, topic, products, companies, for instance) can help break down large indexes into smaller, more readable pieces.

- Check into a variety of Web authoring programs and Web indexing programs, but do not expect these programs to resolve your Web design problems. A good basic knowledge of HTML is essential.

- Do not rely solely on the index to help your visitors find their way around the Web site. A Web site also needs a well-designed navigation system of menus, buttons, image maps, and/or site maps. An on-site search engine may also be of help, because visitors need a choice of ways to access information.

- Price your services fairly. You are providing indexing and Web site design services. An hourly rate is usually necessary because page rates are meaningless in Web indexing. Generally, Web indexers earn $30 to $50/hour, or more. Your client may want to establish an upper limit for the project. Before you agree to a figure, be sure that you and the client are clear on what work is included in the job. Draw up a contract or letter of agreement to specify the Web index preparation and maintenance services you will be providing, as you would in any other indexing project.

- Keep up-to-date on Web indexing methods and strategies and related Web technologies. Do not ignore search engines and methods of combining the two to create a more user-friendly index/search tool. Experiment on your own Web site and other sites you may work on with different types of indexes, site maps, search tools, and navigation systems. Use new technology, but without taxing the computer capability of your "average user." Network with others to share your ideas and learn new ways of creating effective indexes for Web users.

Web indexing is a new and evolving field. Whether Web indexing offers indexers lucrative new work opportunities is still uncertain. Client interest in Web indexing is variable, and Webmasters may be more interested in quick-and-easy search engines than in detailed indexes. But, if this blend of indexing and Web page design appeals to you, take the time to explore the many varieties of Web indexing. No single solution will work for every site and circumstance. Examine as many samples of Web indexing as you can, but do not feel constrained by the indexes you may find online. Use your imagination—develop a new indexing technique that meets the needs both users and indexer-Webmasters in this new and always changing medium.

RESOURCES

Acxiom Corporation: *Case-in-Point* **index,** http://www.acxiom.com/caseinpoint/. This site includes both a search tool and an index. The search engine searches a wider range-of Web site articles and documents than featured in the index, which includes only Case-inPoint newsletter articles, reports, and case studies. The *Case-in-Point* index won second prize in the Australian Society of Indexer Web Indexing contest.

American Society of Indexers Web Site: Indexing the Web,
http://www.ASIndexing.org/webndx.htm. This page offers an overview of back-of-the-book style Web indexing, with links to examples.

Australian Society of Indexers, http://www.zeta.org.au/~aussi/. The Australian Society of Indexers offers an annual Web Indexing Prize. The site provides information on the contest and on past winners.

Part 3
Special Topics in
Computer-Based Indexing

Chapter 7

\<META\> Tags

Marilyn J. Rowland © 1999

<META> tags are used to create meta-information, or information about the information in a Web site. There are many types of <META> tags, but those most relevant to indexing are the description and keyword tags. Description tags provide a short summary of the site contents that are often displayed by search engines when they list search results. Keyword tags are used to define words or phrases that someone using a search engine might use to look for relevant sites. <META> tags are of interest to indexers for two reasons. They provide a means of making your indexing business Web site more visible to those searching the Web for indexing services, and they offer indexers a potential new source of work: writing keyword and description tags for Web site developers and companies with Web sites. <META> tag writing makes good use of an indexer's ability to choose relevant key terms, and the closely related skill of abstracting: conveying the essence of a document in a sentence or two.

\<META\> TAGS AND SEARCH ENGINES

Search engines work by creating indexed references to Web pages. These references contain the title of the page, the URL, a summary description, and a list of keywords. Different search engines choose the summary information and keywords differently and usually combine information from the page's <META> tags with other information from the page. You can overuse <META> tags or use them incorrectly, causing a search engine to ignore your site altogether. Some Web site designers try to trick search engines by using unrelated, but popular terms for keywords (competitor brand names and sex-related terms fall into this category) to attract people to their sites. Because of this potential for misuse, some search engines do not place any weight on the keywords defined in <META> tags and, instead, index the text in the body of the page.

Still, using <META> tags does have some benefits and is generally worth the small effort it takes to create these tags. Search engines that use <META> tags to boost a site's rank in search results include HotBot and Infoseek. Other search engines, such as AltaVista, Excite, and WebCrawler, support <META> tags but do not, necessarily, rank your site any higher because of them.

Do not rely on <META> tags alone to bring your Web site to the top of the list of 463,987 sites listed up by search engines in response to a simple query for indexers. There are numerous other ways to improve your site's standing in the search results, and <META> tags should be used in conjunction with them. Look into several different methods if you are intent on being listed in the top ten sites. See the Resources at the end of this article for some ideas.

WHAT ARE <META> TAGS?

Unlike most HTML tags, <META> tags are used to provide information about a Web site, not to format information on a page. They are non-displaying, or hidden, tags used by browsers and search engines for a multitude of purposes. The Keywords and the Description <META> tags that we will discuss are only two of many such tags. (If you are interested in learning more about other types of <META> tags, check an up-to-date HTML reference book, see the references at the end of this chapter, or search the Web for articles and tutorials.)

<META> Keywords tags contain keywords that describe your Web page. <META> Description tags contain a description of your site or services. This is where your indexing skills come in. You choose the keywords and write a concise description. There is no controlled list of vocabulary terms to which you have to adhere. The process of writing keywords is similar to the usual indexing process, except that all the words are strung together in the keyword tag, in no particular order and without defined subentries.

As in traditional indexing you always need to keep the user in mind. What keywords or combinations of keywords is the user going to choose to find information on your site? What terms would you, an experienced Web aficionado, type into your favorite search engine if you were looking for this site? And what terms might your Web-phobic next-door neighbor use, if he needed to find this information?

You may want to include common variants, British spellings, and misspellings of your keywords. If, for instance, one of your keywords is "archaeology," you might also want to include "archeology"; if one of your keywords is "millennium," you might also want to include "millenium" and "milennium."

The only guidelines are that the keywords should occupy no more than 800-1,000 characters, and keywords should not be repeated over and over again. Some search engines penalize you for repeating keywords by not listing your site at all. One rule of thumb is to use a keyword no more than seven times, either by itself or in combination with another word. For instance, an indexer might use: "indexing, indexer, medical indexing, embedded indexing, scientific indexing, book indexing, and back-of-the-book indexing" but any further use of the word "indexing" may cause search engines to ignore the site.

<META> Description tags allow you to clearly and concisely describe the nature of your site. Your abstracting and summarizing skills will come in handy here. This tag is useful because it gives an exact description of your page to the search engine. The search engine can then use your description when it brings your site up on the search results page. Without description tags, the search engine may write its own description or simply use the first sentence or two from your Web page.

Your description tag should be 200 or fewer characters.

HOW CAN I CREATE <META> TAGS FOR MY INDEXING WEB SITE?

Coding for <META> tags is relatively simple if you are familiar with basic HTML. <META> tags are placed within the <HEAD> section of the page. They have two attributes: NAME and CONTENT. The NAME attribute is used to describe the type of meta-information you are providing (the type of <META> tag you are using). The CONTENT tag is used to provide the actual information (in this case, the keywords and the description). To create <META> tags, you only have to fill in the blanks in the following code: (The <TITLE> tags are not <META> tags, but are included here because they are also one of the tags included in the <HEAD> section of your page, and the contents of the <TITLE> tags are also used by search engines.)

```
<HEAD>
<TITLE>"_____"</TITLE>
<META NAME="keywords" CONTENT="_
">
<META NAME="description" CONTENT="_____">
</HEAD>
```

Type in the title of your site, a list of keywords describing the site, and a description of your site. Here is an example:

```
<HEAD>
<TITLE>Millennium Indexing: Book, Periodical, and Embedded Indexing of
    Computer Documentation</TITLE>
<META NAME="keywords" content="millennium, index, indexing, indexer,
    indexers, books, periodicals, embedded indexing, indexing, computer doc-
    umentation, freelance, millenium, milennium, meloneum, quality, profes-
    sional, service, technology">
<META NAME="description" content=" Millennium Indexing provides
    professional indexing services for Web and text-based computer docu-
    mentation. We offer a high quality product, state-of-the-art technology, and
    friendly service despite your impossible deadlines.">
</HEAD>
```

Note that keywords can also be included in the <TITLE> tags. Instead of just putting the name of your company in the <TITLE> tag, include your business slogan or a few keywords.

Position this code within <HEAD></HEAD> tags (as shown above) at the top of your page after the <HTML> tag. The <TITLE></TITLE> tags are probably the only tags you have thus far placed within the <HEAD></HEAD> tags, though, if you use an HTML authoring program, your program may have placed some additional <META> tags there to identity itself as the authoring tool and you as the author, and to add content information.

Create <META> tags for your home page and top level pages; include all your pages if your site is fairly small or if they contain unique content. Tailor your keywords and description to the individual page, rather than using the same keywords and descriptions for all your pages.

WHAT TOOLS ARE AVAILABLE TO HELP ME CREATE AND ANALYZE MY <META> TAGS?

There are many online and downloadable tools that allow you to create and analyze your <META> tags. Because <META> tags are so easy to create, it is not really necessary to invest in a <META> tag generation program; however, these programs are quick, fun to use, and often free. They are often given away as a promotional device by companies offering other ways to boost your Web traffic for a fee. You have to enter your own keywords and description, but the tools write all the pesky HTML tags for you. They usually include their own promotional messages about their products, but you can delete these lines of advertising before inserting the code into your page.

You'll find a number of online tag generation programs that will show you your results instantly on their Web site or email you the results. All you have to do is highlight, copy, and paste the HTML code into your Web page, removing the advertising message or not, as you wish. See the Resources section at the end of this article for someof these programs.

There are also programs that analyze the keywords and descriptions that you have written and give you hints on how to improve your <META> tags. Other programs will actually write your keywords and descriptions for you. These programs are easily downloaded from the Web, some as free demos, and some for a small fee. Again, see the Resources section for more information.

HOW CAN I GET A JOB AS A <META> TAG INDEXER?

Conceivably, a Web site design company could employ an indexer to create <META> tags. Laura Fillmore, president of Open Book Systems in Rockport, MA, suggests that there is a great future for indexers who can create <META> tag listings. She feels that indexers are ideally qualified to create <META> tags and Web indexes because of their understanding of information architecture and how to arrange information in meaningful hierarchies. Although you won't find many job listings for <META> indexers in your local newspaper at present, Fillmore considers this field to offer growing potential for indexers, particularly for those with related HTML skills who know where to look for work and are persistent. A good place to begin is by contacting large Web developers and consultants who create numerous smaller sites. Fillmore suggests that indexers interested in the field of Web indexing contact publishers of STM (science, technical, medical) journals, such as Wiley, Academic, Springer, Carfax, Blackwell, or any publisher that is actively putting its journals online in databases. She sees a growing trend to put these journals online, whether publicly or in private members-only areas. She predicts that these journals will need good, logically constructed <META> tags and Web indexes. Indexers, in her opinion, are the most qualified to take on these jobs.

For more information, please read Laura Fillmore's article on the topic (see Resources at the end of this chapter).

To get a good start on a career in <META> tag and Web indexing, learn as much as you can about <META> tag indexing by creating <META> tags for your own site and your ASI Chapter site. See if you can boost your own site's rating in a search engine's results. Just as with traditional indexing, <META> tag indexing takes a little practice, and it is a good idea to hone your skills before taking on a job as a <META> tag indexer.

RESOURCES

Books

For general information, consult any good HTML reference book, such as Elizabeth Castro's *HTML for the World Wide Web, A Visual QuickStart Guide* (Berkeley, CA: Peachpit Press, 1998) or Laura Lemay's *Teach Yourself Web Publishing with HTML 4 in a Week* (Indianapolis, IN: SAMS, 1998). Both have good information on <META> tags.

For more information on how to increase your Web site's standing in search engine results, consult William R. Stanek's *Increase Your Web Traffic in a Weekend* (Rocklin, CA: Prima Tech, 1998). Check out your local bookstore or one of the online bookstores such as Amazon.com or BarnesandNoble.com.

Web Sites

Many Web sites provide information on <META> tags. You can use a search engine that recognizes <META> tags to find a site where its creators really know how to use <META> tags effectively, or you can try some of the sites I have found helpful:

Dan's Web Tips: Titles, META tags, and Search Engine Robots, http://www.softdisk. com/comp/dan/webtips/titles.html. A useful discussion of <META> tags and how search engines use them.

Megamoney Metatags: Some Tips for End-of Century Indexer Employment, http://www.obs-us.com/obs/english/papers/massindexer.htm. by Laura Fillmore, presented at the 1997 Fall Conference of the Massachusetts Society of Indexers.

META Tag Resources, http://webdeveloper.com/html/html_metatag_res.html. A large collection of articles on <META> tags and how to use them, collected by Web Developer.com.

META Tag Tutorial, Back to Basics: META tags, by Scott Clark, http://www. webdeveloper.com/categories/html/html_metatags.html. A helpful and readable discussion of many types of <META> tags.

<META> The Proper Uses of HTML's Meta Tag, http://www.webresource.net/html/ basics/meta.html. This page, from Webresource.net, discusses the various uses of <META> tags, including redirecting users to other pages, and how search engines use <META> tags.

Metatags, http://www.metatags.net/. A one-page, but useful, overview of <META> tags and how to use them.

Writing Meta Tags for Higher Search Engine and Good Descriptions, http:// www.globalserve.net/~iwb/search_engine/killer.html. Discusses how to choose keywords and how to write <META> tags.

<META> Tag Checking/Analysis/Creation Tools

<META> Tag tools can analyze your <META> tags and give you tips on changes to improve traffic to your site. Some of them provide only the basic Keyword and Description tags in response to your input, while others check your existing tags, or create keywords by analyzing your site.

Meta Medic, http://www.northernwebs.com/set/setsimjr.html. This tool not only analyzes your <META> tags and points out possible problems, but also includes an auto-generation feature to create <META> tags for pages that do not include them.

Meta Tag Builder, http://vancouver-webpages.com/META/mk-metas.html. This tool, with your input, creates HTML code that includes a number of different types of <META> tags (site creator, subject, publisher, contributors, coverage).

MetatagBuilder, http://www.metatagbuilder.com/. You enter your own title, keywords, and description, and your HTML is instantly generated on their Web site. You copy and paste it into your HTML.

SiteUp's Meta-Tag Generator, http://siteup.com/meta.html. This is a free, downloadable program that allows you to check your <META> tags offline.

WebPromote's Meta-Tag Generator, http://metatag.webpromote.com/. Similar to the others, this site allows you to enter your meta information by emailing the completed code to you rather than displaying it on the site.

Chapter 8

Envisioning the Word:
Multimedia CD-ROM Indexing

X Bonnie Woods

If you are an indexer who is accustomed to working in solitude with static words, you might face some big surprises in the production of a multimedia CD-ROM. You will not be working alone. You will not be working from a manuscript. Your dexterity with a dedicated software tool for indexing will be irrelevant. The coding or tagging might not be your worry either, because it will likely be done by members of a separate technical staff.

The CD-ROM can currently hold 660 megabytes of data. Its production is a massive team effort. Because of the sheer volume of data involved, it is unlikely that one indexer working alone can handle the job in a reasonable period of time. The database for the actual index entries is likely to have been designed specifically for the project at hand, so the indexers will learn the software tools on the job. The entire project will probably be onscreen.

So, if you choose to thrust yourself into this teeming amalgam of production, what are the prerequisites and what new things can you expect to learn?

CD-ROM is an amorphous new medium with few rules. Your most important résumé items might be your flexibility, imagination, and love of words. What remains unchanged from traditional back-of-the-book indexing is the need for empathy with the user; you will still need to come up with exactly the right word for the situation. What is new here is the situation: you might learn to envision the words that correspond to non-textual media such as graphics, photos, video clips, and musical passages. And because you will be dealing with vast amounts of textual and sensory data, you might find yourself rethinking the nature and purpose of an index as a whole. CD-ROM production can take many forms; three will be discussed here.

ENCARTA AFRICANA

My experience in CD-ROM indexing is limited to one vast project: *Encarta Africana*, version 1.0, a comprehensive multimedia encyclopedia on the history, geography, and culture of Africa and people of African descent, published by Microsoft in 1999. During a period of about a year, the project had over 60 staff members in

Cambridge, Massachusetts, and another 40 in Redmond, Washington. This included in-house writers, editors, proofreaders, media coordinators, production staff, and technical staff. There were also more than 200 additional outside writers who contributed articles.

The product comprises 2.5 million words of text and more than 2,000 multimedia elements, including photos, videos, audio clips, interactive maps, charts, tables, and virtual tours. The age range of the encyclopedia's target audience is 15 years to adult. The project manager of *Encarta Africana*, Keith Senzel, is based at Microsoft in Redmond. He has kindly helped me with statistics and technical details about the project for this article.

Despite the magnitude of the project, no one had planned to include an index. Furthermore, the budget did not allow for hiring indexers. I began work on *Encarta Africana* in Cambridge as a manuscript editor, progressed through the title of executive editor, and ended up as the executive director of product completion. It was purely coincidental that I had some familiarity with indexing. Luckily, there were enough editors in the various subject areas who could be mobilized to absorb small editorial assignments of an indexing nature. There is no formal index in *Encarta Africana*; rather, there are several decentralized indexes that are based on the project's user interface and driven by the internal search engine.

Generally, a user interface is the technological construct that forms a common boundary between the user of the CD-ROM and the data; it is the software that enables you to interact and communicate with the computer. What saved the *Encarta Africana* project, from an indexer's point of view, was a well-designed user interface. In this case, the interface had been designed and refined with input from indexers long before the project had been launched in Cambridge. It combines traditional elements of an index with those of a table of contents, but, of course, it has no page numbers. There was enough flexibility within this interface for us to find a suitable compromise between having no index and having a great index—a solution that would allow for the best possible ease of use of the CD-ROM, given our budget and staffing limitations.

We did all writing and editorial work on an internal network, with an editing and tracking software designed by Microsoft specifically for this and other Encarta products. All of the coding for the project's text preparation was in SGML; tagging was done by the technical staff. The editorial, technical, media, and production staff members were located on two different floors of a building on the Harvard campus; we transmitted data to each other in an electronic format by means of the Harvard email network.

The work pace was hectic. One day, at the height of our production schedule, I received 158 email messages, and sent out just about as many myself. Eleven people worked on the indexing as time allowed, in addition to their regular editorial work. This happened during the last month of production. We revised, refined, and transmitted index entries via email. (We never referred to the work as "indexing"; most often we called it "working on the category list.") The final month of production was reminiscent of the last crunch in the production process of a book. We could not begin indexing until after our "freeze" date for content; once the content was stable, we had little time before the final ship date.

We worked within the predetermined structure of the user interface to develop viable, decentralized sections of index. We reached what would correspond to second- and third-level entries. The user is able to search for article title (headword), with the added filters of category, multimedia type, time, place, and word.

Visually, the alphabetical list of headwords is displayed on the screen as a column, left of center. A maximum of 14 titles can be shown at a time. You can type in the article name that you are searching, or you can scroll down the list and click on the title for an immediate link to the piece. The greatest limitation was that we could not add large amounts of either explanatory information or subentries to the headword list except for a number of unavoidable double-postings or cross-references.

Double-postings were linked to the same article, as in the case of Magic Johnson and Earvin Johnson. We listed former names of countries on the headword list as cross-references, with links to the present-day names. We discovered that we often needed to invert article titles to make a more appropriate alphabetical entry and to minimize the number of entries beginning with "African…" or "Black…." Some headwords could bear up to the inversion, such as "Languages, Black"; many titles obviously needed to stay intact, as in "Black Power"; and others have less obvious solutions, as in "Black Seminoles," in which cases the subject editor would make the call. Another problem arose because we were publishing a number of previously copyrighted articles, the titles of which had to remain unchanged. We inverted some of these in order to keep them from getting lost in the alphabetical list, but often these wordings were awkward.

The most flexibility for indexing was in the category search. There are geographic breakdowns (Africa; North America; English- and French-speaking Caribbean; Hispanic America and Brazil; etc.), and then there are further breakdowns into many possible categories, such as physical geography; cities and towns; plants and animals; sciences, exploration, and education; social and political movements; sports; religion; arts; etc. Editors were responsible for assigning categories to the articles in their own subject areas. The category filter's usefulness is wholly dependent on the energy that the various editors and production staff could put into the process. For people who were unaccustomed to sifting through hundreds of articles to ascribe category subentries, this was tedious work. Because different editors were covering different subject areas, with varying levels of intensity, there was unevenness. Categories for Africa, for example, might be more complete than the comparable categories for North America.

The time/place categories cover the years from 15 million B.C.E. to the present. During the final three weeks of the project, one person with a background in history devoted herself completely to the task of skimming through thousands of articles to assign time and place locators for the filters. This was her sole job, and it was actual indexing work. She determined time, by specific year or by century; place, by country or by region. She assigned at least one set of locators for each article; but in the longer articles, she often assigned many more. It seemed important that the bulk of the locators be assigned by one person, for consistency. Because she was not experienced as an indexer, she had to learn quickly how to identify a passing reference, and then how to disregard it. This was important, because otherwise the time and place filters would have been too watered-down to be effective. In the last few days she was joined by one of the Latin American writers, who was able to cover the articles in that subject area more quickly.

There is a full text search function. By typing the search word or term, users get a list of all articles in which that word appears. For example, if you type the word "Zambia," you will get a list of 80 articles. The limitation of this search function is obvious.

The combination of filters can work in the following way: To the right of the headword list are buttons for "word search," "category," "multimedia," and "place," and a sliding timeline cursor that users can click and drag to set the beginning and end dates for their search. Say, for example, you want to look at videos from the years 1960 to the present that deal with African history and culture—specifically in the areas of law and politics, and even more specifically for the country of South Africa. By clicking the appropriate buttons for the various filters, and by clicking and dragging the timeline cursor, you will find within seconds that there are two articles with videos that fit your requirements: Nelson Mandela, and Apartheid. Likewise you could find something as specific as articles with audio clips that deal with the slave trade in Hispanic America and Brazil during the years 1650 to 1700.

One limitation of this form of index is that only article titles can be searched. There is no real content indexing within the articles, except for the internal linking of a cross-reference (known during this project as a q.v., for *quo vide*) whenever possible. That is, if the word "Zulu" appears in any article, it becomes an automatic q.v.; the word will appear in a different color, and when it is clicked it will link directly to the article entitled Zulu. When the context of an internal cross-reference appears in the running text, but the actual title of the article is not used, a *See* reference link is enclosed in parentheses. Editors flagged these q.v.'s during the editing process; the text-prepping technical staff coded them later in SGML.

For many months, the media features editor completed all indexing of the interactive maps and virtual tours. These two features show innovative uses of multimedia, providing carefully designed access points to the specific content. The interactive maps include maps of flora, fauna, ethnicities, art and architecture, as well as maps that are geopolitical and topographical. In the flora map, for example, a large map of Africa is on the right side of the screen. It shows elevations and the country boundaries. On the left side of the screen is a column of headwords that pertain to flora. When the user clicks on "Mahogany," for example, all of the countries in which mahogany grows are highlighted. Also, a photo of mahogany appears, with a link to the article and links to related articles.

The interactive virtual tours of six geographic locations show yet another form of map indexing. The tours link 360-degree views of a location with still images and text. For instance, on the Harlem tour there are three vantage points from which a camera shows a continuous photographic sweep of a Harlem setting. One of them shows 125th Street at Eighth Avenue. The user pans to the left or right by moving the mouse accordingly. While this is underway, there is a small, separate two-dimensional street map that indicates which areas are in view. On this map are various points of interest, indicated by small symbols. By clicking on any particular symbol, a balloon of explanatory text appears. This balloon can also include another multimedia element, such as music.

The *Encarta Africana* project as a whole was successful because editors and production staff mobilized to make indexing decisions—even when the staff had no prior indexing experience. The indexing was also dependent on a well-designed user interface and a staff of text-preppers who could rapidly enter the SGML coding. Also, we were blessed with a production manager who had an innate sense for indexing and who could help keep the staff on target. However, the complex project might have been infinitely easier had there been additional staff members who were professional indexers.

MICROSOFT *ENCARTA 98* AND *ENCARTA 99*

In contrast to *Encarta Africana*'s bare-bones attempt at indexing, the Microsoft *Encarta* 98 and *Encarta* 99 CD-ROMs have a whole team of indexers who have produced 800,000 index entries.

The design of *Encarta Africana* is based on the Microsoft *Encarta* prototype, a comprehensive multimedia encyclopedia. I am grateful to Mark Stumpf, Indexing Lead, Learning and Entertainment Business Unit, Microsoft, for information regarding *Encarta* 98 and *Encarta* 99. He coordinated the large indexing team at Microsoft on the *Encarta* products.

Stumpf came to CD-ROM reference publishing by way of his work in user education at Microsoft, which led him to the idea of producing something other than a back-of-the-book index. He says the technology that produces "help" files bears some similarity to indexing, and the issues faced are the same. He feels his work in user education prepared him to cope with the online aspects of indexing this huge project.

Stumpf worked with Design and Management people from the beginning to "design an index presentation that would work with the existing interface, and yet present the index entries with appropriate prominence." The usability testing is a consistent factor in the design process. When the team of indexers produced the earliest version, there were 32,000 articles and 600,000 index entries created within the first year. There are 14,000 media items in the present version, but only about 2,000 of them have been indexed.

Encarta's articles are classified by editors into at least one of 90 or so categories. These categories provided the basis for organizing the index. Rules and procedures for each subject area followed from this, and helped to ensure consistency. They attempted a larger consistency beyond that, when the entire body of entries was stable. They did not use a controlled vocabulary, but tried to develop standards as they went along.

The headwords of the encyclopedia articles form the majority of the level-one entries. The vocabulary for the level-two and level-three entries arise from the specific contexts. In addition to multimedia searches that are similar to those described for *Encarta Africana*, the entire index appears in one scrolling column; users can type in a word that will link them to that part of the index. In the workplace, a custom indexing system designed by Microsoft serves as the large database for storing the indexers' records; it allows for multiple creators and editors of the entries.

At Microsoft there is ongoing development of the natural language query, with input from indexers. This is a search function that "understands" syntax and synonyms. For instance, Stumpf explains, a user can type in a question such as "How many legs does a crab have?" The search engine must be designed to link immediately to the article on "Crab," rather than "Leg." He is candid about his views on indexing:

> Multimedia CD products are where it's at in the publishing world. One can do things there that can't be done anywhere else. And while most of publishing is a low-wage industry, high tech is a relatively high-wage industry. Working in a publishing venture on the fringes of high tech is therefore a better place to be than the core of traditional publishing.

There are annual updates to the *Encarta* project. Stumpf says that unlike the situation in book indexing, these CD-ROM indexers always get another chance at refining and adjusting the work, with the added advantage of input from user feedback studies.

THE HISTORY OF AUSTRALIA

Garry Cousins describes his experience of being the sole indexer for a text-only CD-ROM version of Manning Clark's 2,500-page, six-volume *History of Australia* (see References, below). At the time that Cousins wrote the article, he was halfway though the project.

He and his publisher had agreed that free-text searching would not be an efficient way to navigate around the text, and so he set out to create a comprehensive subject index. Since this large work was a CD-ROM version of a pre-existing publication, Cousins was able to refer to the original index. The reference locators were meaningless in his newly scanned, onscreen text, which had been converted to a single scrollable document, 5,000 screens long. But he did find the old index to be useful in knowing in advance which names would require subheadings.

He used an approach similar to that of Microsoft Word embedded indexing function to create the coded entries. His tags were to be compiled later—and combined with a text search function—by a programmer. He took the paragraph as the basic unit of the text, and at the beginning of each paragraph he inserted, or embedded, each keyword that applied to the paragraph. He indicated the index entry by enclosing it in angle brackets. If the discussion went beyond one paragraph, he would embed the coded keyword at the beginning of each subsequent paragraph until the discussion stopped. If the same subject was mentioned often, he would include a subheading after a colon. He includes the following example of his coding at the beginning of a paragraph, directly followed by the running text:

> <1840s><1850s><moral campaigns><women: moral protection of><Grey,
> George: recommends resumption of immigration>

Through correspondence (December 1998), Cousins provided me with the epilogue to his article on CD-ROM indexing: He completed the project in six months, working on it half time. He had undercharged the client because he greatly underestimated the amount of time for the job. Furthermore, the project was never released as a CD-ROM. Instead, it went into Macquarie Library Pty Ltd's online reference resource. He had no say in the user interface design. The index entries in the present online version can be retrieved only by doing word searches, and it is impossible to browse the index in its entirety. Users can, however, perform Boolean searches; for example, searching for "unemployment" *and* "1850s," and thereby locating entries concerned with unemployment in the 1850s. Cousins states:

> I have not done any CD-ROM indexing since, and would be very reluctant to work the same way again. What online indexers desperately need is some software of a professional standard written specifically for the purpose. The present approach of trying to "mix and match" bits of software which were really written for other purposes is quite unsatisfactory. Nancy Mulvany highlighted this sorry state of affairs in her book *Indexing Books* some five years ago (pp. 277–280), but nothing seems to have changed since then.

PRACTICAL ISSUES—HOW TO GET A JOB

These three types of CD-ROM indexing projects give some indication of the wide-open nature of the field. In the case of *Encarta Africana*, the indexing was considered secondary to the editing, and indexing credentials were initially seen as irrelevant.

Garry Cousins intentionally worked only half time on his CD-ROM project; he spent the other half juggling other work in back-of-the-book indexing so he would not lose his regular clients in the course of the long project.

The large indexing staff at Microsoft is, it is hoped, more indicative of future CD-ROM productions. Most of the *Encarta 98* and *Encarta 99* indexing was done in-house, with some of the work contracted to outsiders. During the editing phases, the outsiders were brought in. In addition to Mark Stumpf's administrative work, there were four full-time indexers and eight additional part-time indexers, over a period of a year. The staff earned $15–25/hour with benefits.

The indexers were chosen from a variety of backgrounds. Most were from the ranks of back-of-the-book indexers, but others had backgrounds in librarianship, editing, or writing. In hiring indexers, Stumph found that an indexer's computer literacy was a great help, but not decisive in making a good CD-ROM indexer. He also found that "experience with online publishing was proven particularly irrelevant." Most useful, he found, was some background with user education or "help" functions.

USER INTERFACE—INDEXERS AS DESIGNERS

The earlier that indexers can become involved in the CD-ROM design process, the more latitude they will have in designing a usable index. I mean very early, when the CD-ROM is still just an idea. Indexers who are accustomed to being the last cog in the production process might find it hard to imagine this early participation. But it is clear that the function of the user interface cannot be easily separated from the function of the index in a CD-ROM. If the user interface is poorly designed, the best index in the world will not make the content of the CD-ROM accessible.

This might require a different approach to indexing—a more proactive involvement with the project. Rather than waiting until the project is almost completed, an indexer might be most effective in the design of the publication's inner structure.

During my discussions with Mark Stumpf, he raised an interesting point: with online tracking systems it is now possible to trace a user's path through a site. We can keep track of all the users' strings in order to analyze the usage patterns on a Web site.

To follow up on this, one might add that although we might make certain assumptions about the importance of having an index in a book, we never really know *how* or *whether* an index is being used. For a book, we cannot measure the reader's eye movements or the thought sequences that go into the process of looking up a word in the index. But now with online tracking, we can learn exactly how people use an index and we can trace what paths they take to arrive at certain destinations.

As documents online become longer, navigation ease within them becomes more and more important for the retrieval of information. This often involves imposing an internal structure on the information. The structure does not change the information content, but it certainly changes the user's *perception* of it. Information architecture is the art of designing and building usable structures of information. It deals with logical designs for organizing and finding information, based on the use of the monitor screen. In a CD-ROM, the index is not only at the beginning or at the end of the text; it can appear anywhere the interface allows. The redesign of the text presentation may bring with it some changes in our expectations for indexes.

THE INDEXING OF IMAGES AND SOUNDS

Multimedia is more than black type on a white page. Content such as photos, speeches, videos, drawings, maps, and music all deserve a place in an index, too. Indexers have been including entries for paintings and maps in the back of the book for a long time. Titles of paintings and names of the artist are simple enough, as are the geographical names as they appear on a map. But what happens when the content of these multimedia elements needs to be indexed?

In the case of *Encarta Africana*, aside from the interactive map features, only some aspects of the multimedia are indexed. The user can find a video or audio element only through the encyclopedia article in which the element appears. For example, one can find the alphabetical list of 84 available articles that contain videos, and one can find a list of videos that appear within each given encyclopedia article, but one cannot find a list of all videos that contain images of, say, African American sports stars. Nor can one find index entries for the actual content of any given video.

It is easy to imagine creating a set of index entries for a speech, because the content could be transcribed into a textual manuscript, and then analyzed word by word. But how would you index a group of non-word–based images or sounds? For example, imagine a situation in which you might need to provide access points for images that have no titles per se; or for passages of music that have no names, but that need to be found by category type—such as all musical segments that contain piano solos. These situations are unimaginable in the context of a book, but are entirely plausible in a CD-ROM or any online context.

SCROLLING YOUR IMAGINATION

One element of *Encarta Africana* (version 1.0) that captured my imagination is in the upper right corner of the screen—a small scrolling index of sorts. It is a brief list of articles, q.v.'s, or Web sites related to the main article on screen. Only one entry from this list shows at a time ("Check out this related *Encarta 99 Africana* subject: …"), then the type rolls slowly upward, as if these were movie credits, and then another q.v. appears. This short list is on a repeat loop that continues in motion as long as the main article is on screen. The movement is subtle, and you can easily miss seeing it consciously. *Subconsciously*, though, who knows…

One could argue that words in a standard book index already move across space—especially when the reader physically turns the page of a book index. There is certainly an element of time and movement involved in this simple action, but the electronic medium provides a different situation altogether.

Designers for online media know that the most exciting characteristic of type on the screen is the added dimension of time. Time is introduced by motion. Paul Kahn and Krzysztof Lenk discuss how the speed, direction, duration, and growing or shrinking variation in type size can have different effects on the reader. Bringing these factors into the context of an index might open a whole new area of symbols and interpretation. Is anyone mildly intrigued by the notion of an index that incorporates the dimension of time? Your index no longer needs to sit still on the page! The possibilities are intriguing.

ENVISIONING THE WORD

In a book, the user can enter systematically into the content through the index. In the two examples of multimedia CD-ROMs discussed here, there are multiple ways of accessing the content, which might include the index. The multiplicity has pros and cons. We have only begun to think about new ways of systematizing the access points in this new onscreen format.

Bella Haas Weinberg notes that information scientists consider the CD-ROM a transitional technology; they predict that everything will eventually be on the Internet. She describes the limitations of CD-ROM technology as it applies to library information networks in her article "Indexing the Millennium: Future Conditional" (see References, below).

The demise of the CD-ROM may indeed be inevitable, especially when multimedia productions become as easily accessible on the Internet as they are now on a CD-ROM. However, it seems that everything online is in a transitional state, as well, at the moment. This might also be said about every aspect of the publishing industry. I suggest that if an indexer has an opportunity to learn about the CD-ROM medium, there is every reason to plunge into it, to see what's what. Simply because there might be multimedia features in place of words does not mean that there is less content to index.

The anchor for the content will always be the word, despite how many multimedia features are involved. The domain of indexers will always be in their power of envisioning the word. Some person will always need to know precisely the right name that describes the category. The person who can envision the right word at the right time will be someone who, above all, loves words and who empathizes with the users of words. This someone is likely to be an indexer.

REFERENCES

Cousins, Garry, "Conceptual Indexing for CD-ROMs: Beyond Free Text Searching" (paper presented at the annual meeting of the Australian Society of Indexers, Robertson, New South Wales, 1996).

Kahn, Paul and Krzysztof Lenk, "Principals of Typography for User Interface Design." *Interactions: New Visions of Human-Computer Interaction* 6 (Nov.–Dec. 1998): 27.

Mulvany, Nancy, *Indexing Books*. Chicago: University of Chicago Press, 1994.

Weinberg, Bella Haas, "Indexing after the Millennium: Future Conditional." *The Indexer*. 21 (Oct. 1998): 63.

Chapter 9

How to Index
Windows-Based Online Help

Susan Holbert

INTRODUCTION

Today, more and more software packages come with online documentation. Some have complete manuals as well. Others have basic documentation on paper and more advanced information online. I recently purchased a computer that came with 20 software programs and not one page of written documentation. More and more, users have to find information by searching online.

Most documentation teams focus on writing and ignore the problems of information retrieval, making information in printed documents difficult to find, and online information impossible to find. With online Help, you cannot browse the documentation. You cannot even browse more than a couple of inches of the index at a time. If online users do not get superb guidance into the jungle of online Help, they go away like the hero of Joseph Conrad's *Heart of Darkness*, saying "Oh, the horror! The horror!"

How does an online Help index work? The following examples are based on the Windows 95 Help-type system, but do not represent actual Help screens.

To use online Help, you open the Help menu and click Help Topics. Click the Index tab. A window similar to the following appears. Remember, this is only a hypothetical example. You will not be able to find this on your system (**boldface** indicates the highlighted keyword).

CONTENTS (INDEX (FIND (ANSWER WIZARD

1. Type the first few letters of the word you are looking for:

Database

2. Click the entry you want and then click Display

Database program **creating forms** creating tables creating queries

```
importing and exporting data
inserting tables and queries
linking data from multiple tables
linking to external data
mail merge
printing reports
Date
DATE command
field
formatting
inserting into headers and footers
Default settings
automating
```

DISPLAY   PRINT   CANCEL

In the first box (the search box), you type in the subject you are looking for. This takes you to that entry in the second box, where you see a list of 17 keywords, both main entries and subentries. When you highlight a keyword and click Display, one of two things happens. If there is only one Help Topic associated with the keyword, the Help Topic appears. If there are multiple Help Topics, a list of Topics Found appears, containing the titles of all associated Help Topics, as below (**boldface** indicates the highlighted topic):

```
TOPICS FOUND
```

Click a topic, then click **DISPLAY**

```
How To Set Date Options
How To Set Editing Options
How To Set Fonts
How To Set Margins
How To Set Network Options
How To Set Printing Options
How To Set Save Options
How To Set Spelling Options
How To Set Tabs
How To Set View Options
```

DISPLAY   PRINT   CANCEL

When you highlight one of the Topics Found and click Display, the associated Help Topic, also called a Help screen, appears. This screen provides instructions for carrying out the requested task:

> Help Topics | Back | Options
> **How To Set Fonts**
> (1) From the Format Menu, choose Font.
> (2) Type in the name of the font you want or scroll through the list of fonts.
> (3) Samples appear in the Sample box
> (4) Double-click the font name.

This structure allows for up to three indexing levels: main entry keywords, subentry keywords, and Help Topic titles. Each can be used to guide the user to the appropriate Help Topic.

HOW IS AN ONLINE HELP INDEX CREATED?

Each Help Topic exists as a separate unit, linked to the Help index by embedded keywords, which become the index entries. There are a number of software tools for writing online Help, including special purpose programs such as Robo-HELP and Doc-to-help, which are used with Microsoft Word, and full-featured authoring programs such as Framemaker and Interleaf. These programs have online Help writing features; most are fairly expensive, ranging from about $450 to $900, but they are necessary tools for this job. (See Resources at the end of this chapter for more information.) These programs allow the writer or indexer to embed keywords in each Help Topic in two ways.

First, the indexer can prepare a list of target keywords. The software automatically embeds those keywords in every Help Topic in which they appear and creates an index from those keywords. For example, if Printer is a target word, the software will embed the word Printer as a keyword in each Topic that includes the word Printer. When the user goes to the index and selects the keyword Printer, all of those Topics will appear in the Topics Found box. This method creates an index with many trivial and inappropriate references, missed paraphrases, and no cross-references—in short, a very poor index. Even though most programs allow the indexer to say yes or no to each inclusion, doing so takes more time than indexing the document manually.

With the second method, the indexer reads each Help Topic and manually embeds keywords for each Topic. The software creates an index from only those keywords that are embedded in the Topics. Thus the word Printer may appear in a Topic called *Formatting Documents*, but unless the indexer has included Printer as an embedded keyword, clicking on Printer in the index will not lead to the *Formatting Documents* Help screen.

The indexer may also include all Help Topic titles in the index in conjunction with either of these methods. This is helpful only if the writer has written Topic titles with information retrieval in mind. A list of twenty entries beginning with the word About is not helpful.

Indexing Help Topics is more difficult than indexing printed manuals because it is harder to see and review the overall structure of the document. To compound this difficulty, most Help files are written and indexed by a team. The merged indexes are often confusing, disorganized, inconsistent, and repetitive.

THE PRODUCT-ORIENTED VS. THE TASK-ORIENTED INDEX

Online Help users differ from book readers in several important ways. Online users:

- have not read the Help Topics before searching for information
- are unfamiliar with at least some of the terms used
- have as their primary goal doing a task, not reading the documentation

For these reasons, users need a task-oriented rather than a product-oriented index.

Product-oriented indexers concentrate on what the product does. They summarize the information on the page and describe the features that the software offers. When selecting entries, product-oriented indexers ask, "What features are being described?" The index is often a list of commands and chapter headings that users are not familiar with because they have not read the documentation.

Task-oriented indexers concentrate on what users do. When selecting entries, the indexer asks, "What task is the user trying to perform?" Task-oriented indexers do more than just summarize the text. They add terms that describe the procedure from the user's point of view. These terms may be technical and non-technical synonyms, common vocabulary from the workplace, or widely used terms from other products. Some will be in the manual. Others will not. The following sentence is an example:

"To use WordWise files in other programs, save them in non-document mode."

Product-oriented indexers ask, "What does the product do?" Their index includes the following keywords:

Files: saving

Modes: non-document

Non-document mode

Saving: in non-document mode

Task-oriented indexers ask, "What is the user trying to do? Why would a user want to save in non-document mode?" They decide the user is trying to transfer files between programs. Their index includes the following keywords:

Files: transferring
Exporting files
Importing files
Transferring files

If indexers have a technical audience familiar with other terms in the industry, they might also include:

ASCII files
Text files

INDEXING RULES APPLY

When indexing online Help, the basic rules of indexing apply.

- Use multiple points of access; for example, put information about italics under Italics, Fonts, Formatting.

- Create entries for both command names and what the command does; for example, list RD command and also Reference Density.

- Use terms from the workplace; for example, list Reference Density and also Viscosity, if that is a common workplace term.

- Use the most important word for the entry; for example, use Depreciation Functions, not Working with Depreciation Functions.

- Do not be too general or too specific; for example, avoid entries like Creating, Changing, Dialog Boxes.

Editing an online index is even more important than editing a printed index. Take special care to ensure the entries are general enough to include chunks of information. Make sure all related references are listed under one main entry, such as Reference Density, rather than scattered among several, such as Reference Density, Viscosity, and RD Command.

ONLINE DIFFERENCES

In addition to applying the basic rules of indexing, special consideration must be given to screen size, organization of Topics, and the user's inability to scan the keyword list.

Screen Limitations

Keep in mind what the Help system looks like. In Windows 95, only 17 keywords (whether main entries or subentries) can be seen at one time. Each of these keywords can lead to a list of Topics Found that are hidden as the user browses the index. When the user displays the Topics Found, only ten Topic titles can be seen at one time.

Do not make the user scroll up and down or click back and forth comparing related entries to see all available information. Organize your entries so that no subject has more than seventeen adjacent keywords and no keyword is attached to more than ten Help Topics.

The best way to reduce the number of keywords is to ensure sure they are general enough. The example below shows the excessive use of subheadings for the main entry "Documents." Each keyword (Index entry) is embedded in the Help Topic listed across from it. The user has to scroll down a long list (I've seen up to 87 lines!) to browse this single entry and must click Display eighteen times to view all Topics titles under Topics Found.

Index entry (keyword):	Help Topic found:
Documents	About Files
borders	Borders and Patterns
copying text	Copying text (Edit Menu)
cutting	Moving text (Edit Menu)
headers and footer	Headers and Footers
margins	Margins
memory error messages	Error Messages
memory management	Memory Limitations
memory troubleshooting	Troubleshooting
moving text	Moving text (Edit Menu)
Paste Special	commandImporting text (Edit Menu)
pasting	Copying text (Edit Menu)
saving	Saving Files
saving in non-document mode	Transferring Files
saving new files	Saving Files
saving on network	Networked Files
saving with new name	Naming Files
setting tabs	Setting Tabs

In the example below, four general subentries are used to organize related Help Topics. The Topic titles that appear under Topics Found are efficiently utilized to inform the user of more specific information. This entry makes it easier for the user to read the index and to target which subentry will have the desired information.

Index entry (keyword):	Help Topics found:
Documents	About Files
editing	Copying text (Edit Menu)
	Importing text (Edit Menu)
	Moving text (Edit Menu)
formatting	Borders and Patterns
	Headers and Footers

formatting *cont'd.*	Margins
	Setting Tabs
saving	Naming Files
	Networked Files
	Saving Files
	Transferring Files
memory management	Error Messages
	Memory Limitations
	Troubleshooting

Several other good indexing practices can reduce the number of clicks necessary to see relevant information.

- Do not embed alphabetically adjacent keywords in the same Help Topic; for example, in a Help Topic that discusses metric conversion, do not embed Metrics, Metric Conversion, and Meters to Feet.

- Choose one keyword for that alphabetic place in the index. Other embedded keywords should begin with other letters of the alphabet; for example, Converting, Feet to Meters, Kilos, Metric Conversion, and Pounds.

- Try to use one keyword for related word forms; for example, it is easier for the user to review all subentries under Location than to look under Locating, Location, Location search, and Locations.

SOFTWARE LIMITATIONS

It takes many clicks to get to each Help screen and see what is there. Take extra care in selecting informative keywords and Topic titles.

You cannot create freestanding cross-references in the Windows 95 Help system. Every keyword must be embedded in a Topic. To simulate cross-references, you can include a cross-reference in a keyword. For example, you may have several Topics about Reference Density, which is also referred to as Viscosity. You can embed the keyword phrase "Viscosity. *See also* Reference Density" in one of those Topics (for example, *About Reference Density*). Thus the user who goes to Viscosity can display one Topic directly or go immediately to the cross-reference by typing Reference Density into the search box. The following is an example:

Index entry (keyword):	**Help Topics found:**
Viscosity. See also Reference Density	About Reference Density
Reference Density	About Reference Density
	Metric Conversion
	Setting Reference Density

Marketplace Limitations

Online Help indexes are usually created by staff technical writers, editors, and indexers, rather than freelance indexers, though sometimes contract indexers are hired. Freelance indexers looking for this type of work should contact software company documentation departments for more information.

The documentation marketplace is a highly competitive, high-pressure environment with demanding deadlines. Indexes are usually the last item on the production list, and many managers and writers think of them as an afterthought rather than as an integral part of the process. This presents the indexers with two problems that are widespread in the industry.

The first is that there is rarely sufficient time allocated to create a truly useful index. The only solution to this problem is for indexers to continually educate clients about the importance of information retrieval with online documentation.

The second is that it is even more rare for Help Topics to be written with information retrieval in mind. Learning involves three levels of information: overviews, processes, and facts. A good Help system should include overview screens that show the user how the information is organized and process links that lead users to related Topics. Instead, most Help Topics are small fact screens that require users to consult several Topics to get adequate information. Thus the indexer's job, organizing the keywords that lead users to be led to all relevant information on a topic, is both more difficult and more important.

Last, writers rarely write Topic titles to serve as informative subentries or subsubentries. I've seen some so long that the whole title cannot even be viewed in the Topics Found box. Thus the keywords must serve to make distinctions that are not apparent from the Topic titles. Technical writers/indexers of Online Help can help improve the index and the indexing process by becoming more aware of how the documentation affects the index. By taking time to write informative Topic titles and content, the writer, and, especially the writer/indexer, can help improve the quality of the index.

CONCLUSION

Whether we love it or hate it, online documentation is a necessary tool. Knowledgeable indexers can alleviate the difficulty of working with online Help by applying good indexing practices to information retrieval and by working around the inherent limitations of limited screen size, inability to browse, and the repeated clicking necessary to navigate Help screens. The challenges of indexing online Help are many, but the reward is great—knowing that you have made life a little easier for countless frustrated computer users.

RESOURCES

General Sites

Gary Conroy's Mining Company Technical Writing Site, http://techwriting.miningco. com/msub7.htm. A variety of resources for technical writers and authors of online Help.

HTML Writer's Guild, http://www.hwg.org/. A large international organization, the HTML Writers Guild has over 85,000 members. Its goal is:

"to help members to develop and enhance their capabilities as Web authors, to compile and publicize information about standards, practices, techniques, competency, and ethics as applied to Web authoring, and to contribute to the development of the Web and Web technical standards and guidelines."

Online Help Resources, http://members.aol.com/LindaMoore/helpauth.html. Compiled by Linda Moore, this is an excellent, comprehensive and up-to-date listing of links to major online Help authoring sites, discussions, workshops, etc.

Help System Authoring Tools (all are costly)

Doc-To-Help 4, Wextech Systems, Inc. http://www.wextech.com. Doc-To-Help (Version 4 is the most recent) is an add-on to Microsoft Word 95 and 97 that helps the user write Help programs for a variety of platforms, including HTML-based systems. This software allows you to both write and index online Help systems.

Help Magician Pro 4.5, StateLine Software http://helpmagician.com/. A WYSIWYG Help and Web site authoring program.

RoboHELP Office 7, Blue Sky Software http://www.blue-sky.com. Also expensive, RoboHELP allows you create Help files for all major formats and produce Intranet information systems. It includes an Index Designer that allows you to create an index and a Smart Index that can automatically generate an index from your text files.

Win Help/HTML Help, http://www.hyperact.com/hyperac8.html. A site that directs you to a variety of resources about this Microsoft-based Help authoring programs.

Part 4
Beyond Traditional Marketing—
Selling Yourself in Hyperspace

Chapter 10

Web Site Design for Indexers

Marilyn J. Rowland

DO INDEXERS REALLY NEED WEB SITES?

No, they do not. Indexers do not need computers either. Indexes can be done on cards; networking can be done at conferences; and marketing can be done with cold calls. But, just as email has become indispensable to communication, and computers have become essential to indexing, so Web sites have become more and more necessary for all types of businesses, particularly small companies with small advertising budgets, like indexing businesses. The amount of business being conducted on the Web is increasing exponentially. Publishers, packagers, and other potential clients are beginning to search the Web for indexers. Why not participate in e-commerce, the newest way of doing business?

A good Web site not only helps you obtain work, it increases your professional reputation and helps you influence the future of indexing. You can use your site as an online resume, to display a list of all the books you have indexed in the past year, to provide examples of your work, and to network with others. You can use it to express your philosophy of indexing, to teach others about indexing, and to make your voice heard on issues affecting the indexing profession.

Not all indexers need Web sites, but active, involved, and far-sighted indexers, like you, do!

WILL A WEB SITE BRING ME LOTS OF NEW INDEXING BUSINESS?

No, not if you expect to create a Web site and then sit back and wait for email requests for your services to pour in. You have to use your Web site as part of your overall business plan and marketing activities.

The first step is to let people know about your Web site. There are many ways to do this. Use your Web site address in your email signature. Put it on your letterhead and business cards and in your listings in professional association member directories. Feature it prominently in your advertising.

Tell all who will listen that you have a Web site. List it on the search engines. Be sure you have included <META> tags to help search engines find your site. (See "<META> Tags," Chapter 7.) Encourage other people to link their sites to your site. Link to theirs. Make sure your Web site draws people to it. Post a great article about indexing, a comprehensive list of resources of interest to indexers, an interactive crossword puzzle, a checklist or quiz on how to evaluate an index, or even a selection of quick and easy recipes for deadline crunch days.

Gradually people will visit your site, and eventually your efforts will pay off. In all likelihood, other indexers will notice it first. Based on your online presentation, they may write to ask you for help in starting their indexing careers, or they may refer work to you, feeling confident of your professionalism. Networking is crucial to your own business development and to the growth of the profession of indexing, and it will also bring you new clients.

WHAT HARDWARE AND SOFTWARE DO I NEED?

You can create a Web site with nothing more than a text editor such as Notepad or WordPad, or a shareware HTML editing program; an Internet service provider (ISP) or commercial online service account; and an FTP program to send the files to your server.

You can also spend thousands buying state-of-the-art hardware and software to create elaborate multimedia Web sites. You may also decide to buy space on a server to supplement your ISP space and/or to provide additional capability to handle your growing needs.

At a bare-minimum (not counting hardware, ISP, or your time), you will need a couple of software programs, a couple of books, a night-school class on HTML, and your business logo scanned for use on the Web. Costs might amount to $200, $500, or even $1,000, depending on your needs and your willingness to spend money.

Let's assume that you want to keep costs to a minimum, at least at first. There is a lot you can do with free and inexpensive software, but if you are planning to use graphics and multimedia, your expenses may rise. You may want to buy a scanner, for instance, or a high-end Web authoring program or two. Inevitably, you'll want to spend more to upgrade your hardware and software six months down the road when rapidly changing Web technology changes again!

Web Authoring Tools

You do not absolutely need Web authoring tools, and some people, including professional Web site designers, prefer not to use them at all. You can create colorful and elaborate Web sites with a text editor and a knowledge of HTML. But authoring tools can be enormously helpful and time saving, particularly if you are used to working in a "What You See Is What You Get" (WYSIWYG) environment. You can create Web sites entirely within WYSIWYG environments without having to deal with HTML code directly, and this makes the job of creating a Web site similar to word processing or desktop publishing.

Despite the advantages built into WYSIWYG Web authoring tools, you will find it worthwhile to take the time to learn basic HTML language. With a better understanding of how HTML works, you will have the knowledge to resolve those vexing coding problems that are always popping up, even in the WYSIWYG environment.

A wide range of programs are available for the Web page designer. In addition to WYSIWYG programs, you'll find straight HTML programs and sophisticated page design and administration programs, as well as all types of add-ons, utilities, and special-purpose software. Though you can spend $100 to $3,000 on such programs, many shareware, freeware, and demo programs are yours for the downloading. Start with a free program such as Netscape Communicator's Composer, which comes in the full download of the Netscape browser. This program, like other free and low-cost software, generally has all the features a new Web designer needs and can help you decide what features you might want in a more expensive program.

Choosing software, even among free products, can be a little overwhelming. Several useful Web sites for product comparisons, reviews, and downloads are listed in the Resources at the end of this article.

Graphics Programs

The right graphics, whether informative, entertaining, or simply decorative, add a lot to a Web site. You can use free and commercially available clip art on your site, but a better solution is to create your own art. Even if you are not an artist, you can do a lot with a paint program and some patience. Try creating and combining some simple geometric designs in a basic paint program instead of using ready-made clip art. You can also scan photos and original artwork and/or commission a Web artist to create something exactly right for your page.

PhotoShop is the program of choice among Web designers. However, it costs $500-600, so the casual Web site creator might want to consider PaintShopPro, which is available free as a demo or for about $60, or similar graphics programs.

Multimedia Programs

You can enliven your basic Web site with multimedia. While you want to be careful not to overwhelm your visitors with irritating geegaws that require them to download plug-ins before they can see them, or detract from the information you are trying to convey through your site, you may want to consider some simple animated graphics, image maps, and techniques using JavaScript. Some simple and sophisticated programs are offered as shareware or demo programs.

Hardware

You do not need a state-of-the-art computer to write HTML code and create and upload a basic Web page, but if you surf the Web much, or if you plan to use graphics or multimedia, you will need an up-to-date computer with plenty of RAM and hard disk space, and a high-speed modem, ISDN (internet service digital network) line, or cable modem. A large (17- or 20-inch) monitor is highly desirable. If you plan to create your own graphics, you'll want a scanner and/or a digital camera. Total hardware costs might be $1,200 to 5,000, if you are starting from scratch.

Books and Tutorials

As any computer book indexer knows, there are dozens of new books about the Web published every day, completely outdating the books you bought yesterday. Web books typically range in price from $20 to 50. Most come with CDs full of shareware programs and files. Look for discounts. For an up-to-date list of available books, often with reviews, check one of the online bookstores, such as Amazon.com and BarnesandNoble.com.

Classes and Workshops

Many colleges and universities offer classes in various aspects of Web site design and programming. You may also find basic training through your community's adult education program, special workshops offered by chambers of commerce, economic development groups, and professional societies. Computer and Internet conventions or expositions offer short workshops, and some companies and consultants specialize in such courses. Courses vary in price from free to $1,000.

There are also tutorials and FAQs (frequently asked questions) available right on the Web. Tutorials on the Web are usually free and can be very helpful.

Internet Service Providers (ISPs) and Servers

There are many ways to access the Internet and many options for obtaining space for your Web site, including online services, local or national ISPs, Web malls, and even Web TV. You'll need to consider what you want in a Web site and which providers offer the best features for you, at the best cost.

Monthly costs for unlimited access to the Internet through commercial online services and ISPs range from about $10 to $30 a month for basic services, though free sites are also available if you are willing to accept the advertising that accompanies them. Generally, costs are higher for ISPs, which offer a full range of Web site support services. If you need a substantial amount of space for your Web site or need support for special features, such as online commerce or online databases, you should consider buying space on a specialized server. Such servers provide space and service only; you will still need an ISP or commercial online service to access the server and for email service. Server space starts at about $10 a month.

Domain Names

Virtual domain names allow you to create your own Web site name. Instead of an address like www.onlineservice.com/members/yourname, you can have the more elegant www.yourname.com. You'll have an easier address to remember, and your business will look more professional.

Domain names cost $70 for two years; there may also be an extra monthly billing from your ISP or server to administer your virtual domain. Most ISPs or servers will handle, or walk you through, the procedures necessary to obtain a domain name.

HOW DO I CREATE MY WEB SITE?

Defining its Purpose

The first step in creating your Web site is to clearly define its purpose. What are you trying to accomplish with your Web site? Do you want a professional site, a personal site, or some combination of the two? Do you want to advertise your skills as an indexer, or do you want to meet other indexers who index ancient history textbooks or like to water ski?

The purpose of a commercial site is clear if you are selling indexing software or T-shirts with an indexing motif, but is less easily defined if you are selling indexing services. You are, essentially, selling yourself, your expertise, and your ability to meet your client's needs. If your site is intended as part of your marketing efforts, make it a professional site. Leave out the photos of your family and your pets. Sell your professional skills and knowledge.

Write down your goals for your site and keep them in mind as you proceed through the process of planning and designing your site.

Identifying Your Audience

Any good indexer knows the importance of considering the audience for your project. The same advice holds true in Web site design. For whom are you designing the site? You may be most interested in appealing to publishers and other potential clients, fellow indexers, or people wanting to learn more about indexing; or you may be most interested in expressing yourself by publishing your ideas about indexing and thoughts on life.

If your primary purpose is to advertise your business and attract new clients, your site may look quite unlike the site of someone who wants to experiment with all the latest Web techniques. If your primary goal is to share photos and funny stories about your cats with fellow indexers, you will have an entirely different site from someone who wants to address the philosophical issues of subheading indentation.

Other indexers will be most likely to look at your site, especially if you offer them articles of interest and/or links to online resources they can use. It is fine to orient your site primarily to other indexers. Actually, you may find that you get as much work from other indexers, either directly, or through referrals, as you do from publishers.

What to Include on Your Site

For purposes of this article, let us imagine your audience consists of potential clients, other indexers, and would-be indexers. This audience is interested in your professional qualifications and the information and expertise you may have to offer on indexing.

You may want to include the following elements in your site:
- resume/background information
- list of services offered
- promotional information (why someone should hire you over another indexer)
- list of books, periodicals, Web sites, CD-ROMs, and other material indexed
- names of clients and links to client sites
- other experience (editorial and writing services, abstracting, television production)
- articles on various aspects of indexing
- FAQs (frequently asked questions) about matters related to indexing, writing, publishing, or the Internet
- advice for other indexers, would-be indexers, new indexers, or clients
- sample indexes or portions of indexes
- calendar of events of interest to indexers (local and national ASI events, for instance)
- an interactive bulletin board
- links to Web sites of others indexers
- links to other indexing resources, including the national ASI site (asindexing. org) and local ASI chapters
- an online index to your site (to help visitors navigate your site and to demonstrate your indexing skills)

You may want to *omit* the following elements in your site:
- links to your favorite non-indexing sites (My Favorite UFO sites, for instance)
- out-of-focus or poorly cropped photos
- photos of you in non-professional settings
- photos of your pets (even an adorable iguana warming itself on the top of your monitor)
- persistent animation; busy backgrounds, distracting color schemes
- large, slow-to-download graphics
- graphics or elements that require visitors to download an unusual plug-in before they can gain entrance to your site

- cliché clip art, that stuff you've seen before
- articles railing against the most horrible client ever

Don't be too proper though. Let your uniqueness shine through. Sometimes, just as in real life, it is that odd personal element that draws one person to another. You may indeed get an indexing job because the client appreciates your peculiar link to a recipe for cheesecake.

If you have something you want to sell on the Web (an indexing course, a booklet, software, or coffee mugs showing an indexer staring blearily at a computer screen), you will want to include an order form, and perhaps, if you are offering many items, a searchable catalog.

Many indexers also perform other types of editorial work, writing, and/or computer-related work, such as Web page design. You may want to list all your skills and talents in the same Web site, or you may want to create several linked sites to better highlight the many services you offer.

The great advantage a Web site offers over print media is that you can always change your mind about the contents, presentation, and organization of your site. You can add new features, remove older ones, correct a typo, or totally reorganize the site. Setup a schedule to keep your site fresh by reviewing, adding, and deleting features once a month or every quarter.

As technology changes, you may want to take advantage of new capabilities. Be aware, though, that many Web users will be accessing the site from older computers lacking advanced multimedia features, or even color monitors. Take care to design a site that will look good through a variety of browsers, even dated browsers on antique equipment. This means you should limit use of cutting-edge technology, unless you are willing to create two sites, one for older computers and browsers, and one for state-of-the-art systems.

Pay attention to your writing style, and ask someone to proofread what you have written and evaluate your site from the user's point of view.

CREATING A STRUCTURE FOR YOUR SITE

The structure of a Web site differs from the more familiar structure of books, newsletters, and other publications. Visitors can't pick up a Web site and flip through it to see what might be of interest. They can't assess the size or usefulness of a Web site by looking at the home page or menu buttons. In order to convey information about the contents of your site to visitors, you will have to organize your contents well and provide clear links to various areas of the site. If you want people to use your site, make sure to tell them what's there and how they can get to it.

Plan your site carefully on paper before you start creating pages on the computer. Take pencil in hand and sketch out your pages and the relationships between pages.

First, make a list of all the content elements you want to include in your Web site (a list of services; your article on how to consolidate subheadings; links to the Web sites of other indexers, etc.). Decide which elements might appear on the same page; and which should be on a page by themselves; and which topics might require a whole set of Web pages.

Your thoughtful article on choosing and editing subheadings, for instance, might be logically placed on one Web page, or it might be long enough and complex enough to require five Web pages, especially if you want the article to read like a tutorial. If you are a new indexer, your list of services provided may be combined with your list of clients; if you have many years of experience, your list of services might be a page by itself, linking to specific examples of each type of service. Don't forget your home page. It should describe what your site is all about and what can be found within it.

After you decide on your content elements, organize them in logical categories and develop sub-areas for your Web site: preferably four to six areas that you will provide access to through a menu system.

Sketch the links among your Web pages to indicate structure. What makes sense in terms of your content? What will make navigation easy and logical for your audience? If there is a particular site element you want people to notice (your resume, for instance), how can you attract their attention to it?

For a straightforward site, it is best to make sure that the structure of the site is readily apparent to the viewer. Tell your audience what is in the site and how the information is arranged. Make the structure predictable by using navigation tools, such as a menu, buttons, and/or an index, to help people cruise your site. Each page should have a menu to other main areas of the site; people shouldn't have to return to the home page each time they want to go somewhere else on your site.

A site index can be a great help to users and also show off your indexing skills, but do not force the index to make up for a lack of site organization.

CREATING YOUR SITE

You will need to spend some time learning about HTML tags and how they work. Tags are relatively easy to learn (use <B> and </B> tags, for instance, surrounding text you want boldfaced). There are more than enough books and Web sites and tutorials to assist you. If you want to use special effects on your site, you may want to look into CGI scripts, JavaScript, Java applets, DHTML, XML, Active Server Pages, and other technologies. Limit yourself to simple HTML in the beginning, whether you are writing HTML from scratch or using an HTML authoring program that writes the code for you. After you have created and modified a site or two, you'll probably want to experiment with different types of Web technologies.

MAKING YOUR SITE LOOK GOOD

All your careful work developing and organizing content will count for little if the visual appearance of your site confuses people, bores them, misleads them, or distracts them. Take the time to explore other sites and see what design features make a site work, and what features detract from the visual appearance and/or the usability of the site.

You may deter people with a text-dense page that has words covering every inch of the screen. Your content may be great, but if there are no headings, images, or white space to break the text into digestible chunks, the reader's eyes will glaze over.

You will also chase people away with a graphically intense page. Leave out the large graphics, jarring animations, hard-to-read or unprintable text color schemes, busy backgrounds, and unnecessary clip art. Be original. Your reader will groan if she sees the same pieces of book-related clip art on your page as she did on other indexers' pages.

Your reader wants to learn more about you and about indexing. Make it as easy as possible for him to obtain this information. Good design is more than avoiding bad design. You want to create a page that invites the viewer to explore further and makes it easy for her to do so, and you want your pages to stand out from all the rest.

There are dozens of Web sites and books offering advice and tips on how to design a Web site. Not all these sites and books are themselves well designed, but there is certainly no lack of advice and assistance for the would-be Web designer. Check the Resources at the end of this chapter for a sampling of tips and advice sites.

Look at examples of good and bad design. There are many "Best of the Web" and "Worst of the Web" sites to look at. You may or may not agree with the analyses made by others, but it is often very helpful to hear what professional designers have to say on the topic, and it will help you think about the design process more clearly.

Here are a few design guidelines:

- Web page technology is changing by the minute. Divider lines used to be a major design element; now they identify a site as dated. Resource-intense audio/visual movies on Web sites are almost passé, and those animated mailboxes are curious relics of the past. Keep as up-to-date as you can on the latest features of HTML and related applications so your pages (and therefore your content) do not look dated or unprofessional.

- Do not let yourself get boxed in by HTML restrictions or enticed by the glamour of the latest technology. Design your pages on paper first, and then put your Web skills to work, rather than scrunching your site into some predefined template or HTML tag. It is likely that you will change your ideas many times before you are finished, as you wrestle with HTML limitations, but your design will likely be improved by the time and effort you devote to the task.

- Be creative. Use your own judgment. Do not rely on templates you have purchased or copied from other sites. Examine the HMTL coding in sites you admire, but use the designs of others as inspiration, not as a replacement for your own thinking. Make your own graphics. You don't have to be an artist. You just have to be willing to experiment.

- Make use of white space and text positioning to make your Web pages interesting and reduce visual clutter. Tables and frames can be used creatively to position text.

- When in doubt, minimize the use of space-consuming graphics and other features (sound, video, Java applets) that slow down page loading and may discourage people from looking at your site at all.

- Try to avoid Web clichés. Your site should have a certain ambiance, a sense of overall design, mood, or feeling that conveys a sense of yourself and your work, not just another indexer site.

- Once you design a page, do make your own template for future pages and seek to unify your site through an overall consistency of design elements: page color, background, navigation bars, buttons, lines, and icons. Consistency will add to the visual design of your page and provide visitors with a better sense of how to navigate your site.

- Have fun with your designs and keep your sense of humor, even at 3 a.m. when you can't figure out how to get your perfect graphic positioned properly in your [otherwise] perfect page.

A WEB SITE IS NEVER DONE

Once you've finished your Web site, it is time to revise it, fine-tune it, completely reorganize it, and/or add another few pages. Keep your site up-to-date by adding content and incorporating new Web technology, as appropriate. Check your links now and then to make sure they work. Give people, especially prospective clients, reasons for returning (for instance: new articles and information, useful links, changing content, up-to-date meeting notices).

Promoting Your Site

Make sure your site is listed on all the major search engines. You can submit the URL to each search engine yourself (many search engines have an "Add URL" feature), or use a service (such as Submit-It: http://www.submit-it.com/ or WebPromote: http://www.webpromote.com/) to do this. Depending on how you go about this, the cost for listing your site can vary from nothing (other than your time, which can be considerable) to several hundred dollars.

Let people know about your site by including the URL in your email signature, putting it on your business cards and stationery, including it in advertising, and in ASI and other member directories. Mention it to your clients and colleagues.

If you include links to other indexer's pages on your site, ask them to include a link to your page on their sites. Communicate through your site. Refer current and prospective clients to your site to see your most up-to-date list of books indexed, samples of your work, and/or your recent article on alphabetic order. You can save paper, postage, and time.

Whether your site brings you new clients and lucrative indexing jobs or not, you can use it as a networking tool, as a means of expounding upon your indexing philosophy, and/or as a place to try out new Web design and technology. Have fun with it.

ONLINE RESOURCES FOR WEB SITE DESIGNERS

General Information

CNETBuilder.com, http://home.cnet.com/webbuilding/0-3880.html.. A very informative site, crammed full of information and resources on all aspects of Web site creation, including product reviews and comparisons, and downloads for all levels. Includes information on choosing the right Web authoring tool.

How do they do that with HTML?, http://www.nashville.net/~carl/htmlguide/f-right. html). Tricks and tips on HTML and graphics.

HTML Goodies, http://www.htmlgoodies.com/. Lots of basic information and easy-to-follow tutorials.

HTML Writers Guild, http://www.hwg.org. The WWW Development Resources contains a large and useful collection of links in their Resources section. You can also join the HWG and take HTML classes online.

Internet.com, WebReference, http://www.webreference.com/. Another very informative site, with lots of articles on all aspects of creating Web sites, including emerging Web technology. Many links to tutorials and information on all aspects of Web page development.

WebDeveloper.com., http://www.webdeveloper.com. Articles, software, and book reviews, and lots of resources and links to even more resources.

Web Developers Virtual Library, http://www.stars.com/. A comprehensive illustrated encyclopedia of Web technology, including tutorials, examples, and links to other resources. Topics include HTML, CGI, Java, JavaScript, graphics, VRML, multimedia, animation. See, specifically, their annotated list of Web authoring tools, with links to sources: http://www.stars.com/Vlib/Authoring/HTML_Editors.html

Webmaster-resources, http://www.webmaster-resources.com. Useful information for webmasters at all levels. Contains an annotated list of tools for Webmasters, including links to download sites for free and demo software.

Design Guidelines and Tip Collections

Art and the Zen of Web Sites, http://www.tlc-systems.com/webtips.htm. Lots of good advice on goals, navigation, generating repeat business, color, image maps, page titles, images, loading time, animated images, Java, frames, text, and advertising, told with humor.

Creating Killer Web Sites, http://www.killersites.com/. This site shows examples discussed in the book by the same name. The author significantly influenced Web pages, and has elicited both admiration and criticism. Includes tips for writers and designers.

Dmitry Kirsanov's Top Ten Web Design Tips, http://www.design.ru/ttt/. A good introduction to design. Includes tutorials.

Webling's Web pages design and authoring, http://mvassist.pair.com/Design.html. Links to numerous sites on good and bad Web site design, and a full range of Web topics.

Yale C/AIM Web Style Guide, http://info.med.yale.edu/caim/manual/. A very detailed, very serious guide to page design, graphics, and multimedia.

Chapter 11

Putting Sample Indexes on Your Web Site

Rachel Rice © 1999

Why do you need samples of your indexing work on your Web site? Think about these situations:

Scenario 1: You've contacted a potential client who says he has a project ready to be assigned. He requests some samples of your work. You fax them to him right away and call back a few hours later. "Oh," he says, "I didn't get the fax but anyway I already assigned the project. I can keep your name for future reference, though."

Scenario 2: Another potential client asks you to send her some samples and if they're satisfactory, she'll put you on the freelance list. You mail them to her, or even FedEx them if you can spend the money. You wait a week and call her back. She does not remember who you are, and has not seen the samples. If she can find them, she says, she will file them for future reference.

Scenario 3: You contacted a potential client who has asked to see some samples of your work. As it happens, she has a project ready to go and if your work is acceptable, you can have the job. You can FedEx her some samples, or you can fax them, she says. You think about FedEx and faxing costs, and mail and faxes that never get to her desk, and the risk of losing the assignment if she calls someone else later today, which she almost surely will, and you suggest an alternative. If she has Internet access, she can see a list of the indexes you've completed, and some samples of your indexes instantly. She is impressed that you have the know-how to create a Web site, and agrees to take a look and call you back shortly. You give her your URL and your phone number, and stand by. In five minutes she calls you back, says she is pleased with what she saw, and asks for your address so she can send the job out to you today.

There are obvious advantages to having your work so easily available. However, there are some disadvantages, too. Unless you are very familiar with HTML, it is hard to get your samples to look good in a browser. The formatting might appear odd-looking and can vary from browser to browser, the indentations might be too large, and a potential client might not understand this and think that's how you submit your work. And if your Web site doesn't look professional and is difficult to navigate, you might frustrate your client and be worse off than if you had sent that fax.

But for our purposes, you have decided to go ahead and put your samples up. You've made a list of all your indexes, and you have cleaned up your samples to present an excellent picture of your work and your professionalism. Now you have to get them ready to upload to your site.

WHAT TO INCLUDE ON YOUR SITE

Here's a list of HTML features you might want to include on your Web pages:

- On every page of your site—Home page, Samples page; and on every sample—provide a link to return to your Home page, and a link for someone to send you email.
- On your Home page, provide a link to your Samples page.
- On your Samples page, write a brief introduction stating your indexing background, any specialties you have, how to use the links to your samples.

PREPARING YOUR SAMPLES

There are a number of good HTML editors available, but you don't need one to create your Samples pages, and you don't need to know much HTML. All you need is a word processor. Here's what you need to know:

- You can use paragraph returns in your document to make them easier for you to read in your word processor, but they won't show up when you view your page in a browser. To make an actual paragraph or line break, you must insert a <P> (see below for an explanation of the codes you'll be using).
- You must save your document as Text only (ASCII).
- You must name your documents appropriately.
    - → Name your Home page file index.html (this has nothing to do with indexing as we know it, it's just your Home page)
    - → Name your Samples page samples.html
    - → Name your samples as appropriate, always with the suffix .html. For example, a sample for an index to a book titled How to Buy a Car could be named hbc.html or car.html
    Note: PC users can use the suffix .htm instead of .html

HTML CODES

Here is a list of the codes and what they do. You can use upper or lower case.

On your Home page and Samples page:

<HTML>   goes at the beginning of every document

<HEAD>   creates a larger type size for a heading

<TITLE>   creates the title for the page as it will show in the menu bar in the browser

</TITLE>   signifies the end of the title

</HEAD>   signifies the end of the heading

<BODY>   indicates the main body of your page and creates an appropriate type size

<BODY BGCOLOR="#6BAEBC"> optional code for background color (this is a blue) (you can put this in if you like but I have not used color in our examples)

<H2>   another heading but smaller size

</H2>   signifies the end of that heading

<ADDRESS> formats an area for signatures or general information about a document's author

<A HREF="mailto:Your Email Address">Your Name</A> creates the email link

</ADDRESS> signifies the end of the address section

<HR>   creates an attractive horizontal rule

<P>   creates a hard return for the end of a line or paragraph

<UL>   indicates that you are making a list

<LI>   causes each list item to indent and have a bullet

</UL>   indicates the end of your list

<A HREF="File Name"><EM>Title</EM>(Author)</A>: Publisher. This is the code for a link to an actual sample, where File Name is the name of your document, e.g. hbc.html; Title is the actual title of the book, and obviously the author and publisher are what they are

<A HREF="http://Your Website">The Name of Your Website</A> this creates a link back to your Home page

</HTML>   this must be the last line of your document for any Web page

On your sample:

<DT>   use this for main entries

<DD>   use this for subentries

<I>   start italicized text

</I>   end italicized text

Note that you can also can use <EM></EM> for italicizing

Here's an example of a coded Samples page that you can easily adapt for your own purposes.

```
<HTML>
<HEAD>
<TITLE>        Sample Indexes</TITLE>
</HEAD>
<BODY>
<H2>           Samples of Indexes</H2>
```

Here is a list of recent indexes written by John Jones. Those linked to a sample are highlighted and you can just click on the link to view the sample. Please note that samples are formatted within the limitations of HTML and might look odd in places. For properly formatted samples via fax, attached email, or by regular mail, for job references, or more information about my services, please send a request to <A HREF="MAILTO:jj@somewhere.net">John Jones</A>

```
<HR>
<P>Cats:</P>
<UL>
<LI><A HREF="cac.html"><EM>Cats Are Cool</EM></A> (Bell): MyPress
<LI><EM>All My Cats</EM>(Smith): YourPress
</UL>
<P>Miscellaneous:</P>
<UL>
<LI><EM>Cats and More Cats</EM> (Green): AnotherPress
</UL>
<HR>
```

Return to <A HREF="http://homepage.jjones.somewhere.net/jj">John Jones's Home Page</A>

```
<HR>
<ADDRESS>
```

Send email to <A HREF="mailto:jjones@somewhere.net">John Jones</A>

```
</ADDRESS>
</HTML>
```

Figure 11.1 shows how it will look in your browser, with **boldface** type indicating what would be a hot link on your page. Note that pages will have different appearances in different browsers:

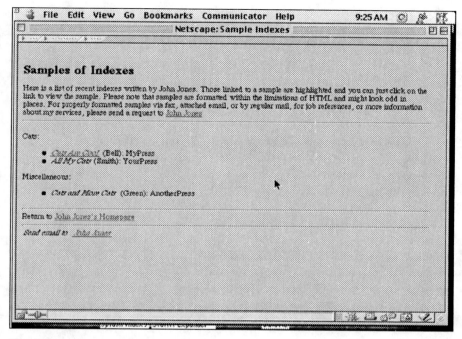

Figure 11.1

Here is a very brief sample index. You can adapt it to create your own sample.

<HTML><P>

<TITLE>Cats Are Cool</title><P<BODY><P>

<P>

Cats Are Cool Index<P>

<P>

A<P>

<DT>adipose cats. <I>See</I> obesity<P>

<DT>adding cats to your household<P>

<DD>adults, 30<P>

<DD>kittens, 148<P>

B<P>

<DT>bringing your cat home. <I>See also</I> adding cats to your
        household<P>

<DT>buying a cat, 146, 164<P>

<DD>equipment needed, 241<P>

<DD>preparation, 240<P>

<DT><HR><P>

<DT>Return to <S HREF="http://Your Home Page">Name of Your Home Page</A><P>

<DT><HR><P>

<DT><ADDRESS><P>

<DT>Send email to <A HREF="MAILTO:Your Email Address">Your Name</A><P>

<DT></ADDRESS><P>

<DT></HTML>

Figure 11.2 shows how it will look in your browser.

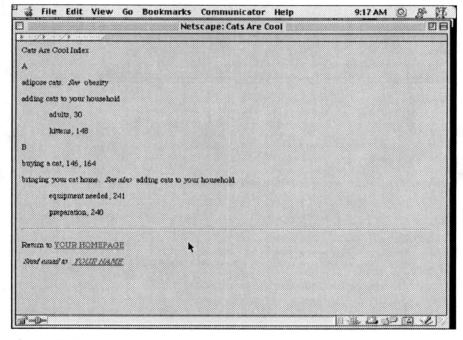

Figure 11.2

And here is a line of code to put on your Home page that will provide a link to your Samples page, provided you have named your document samples.html.

To see how I've constructed my Web site using the information I've presented, take a look at my site:

http://homepages.together.net/~racric/samples.html

There are much more sophisticated ways to construct your site, and of course you can make it much jazzier and snappier. If you come across a site that has a page construction you admire, you can view the codes the author used by selecting Page Source from the view menu of your browser. It will give you all the codes and you can adapt them for your use. Remember that it is illegal to use someone else's designs without permission.

This very basic, simple, and usable option should give you a nice uncluttered and easily navigable Web site that you can be proud to show to your prospective client.

Chapter 12

The Many Uses of Email Discussion Lists

Daniel A. Connolly

INTRODUCTION

If you want to let other indexers know about a great new medical dictionary, discuss the pros and cons of using prepositions in subentries, find an indexer in Phoenix, or maybe share some marketing tips, then consider joining an email discussion list. Email discussion lists provide numerous tools and opportunities for indexers, especially for freelancers.

Despite the rapid growth of Web- and graphical-based communication, email remains the linchpin of electronic communication. While the World Wide Web has become ubiquitous in our society, email remains the most reliable form of electronic communication. Email access is more prevalent than Web access, less cumbersome, and some would say, more egalitarian. Despite improvements over time, Web access is not available in equal quality or proportion to email access, especially in poorer or developing areas. Indeed, many users who have access to both restrict their use of the Web for important research efforts, and maintain near-constant connection with their email servers for daily business.

DEFINITION

A discussion list is an automated system that allows groups of people to communicate via email. Subscribers, or list members, send their messages to the list server; the server then automatically forwards these messages to all other members of the list. There are various list configurations and distribution options, but, essentially, discussion lists connect individuals to others with similar interests. Email discussion lists are extremely flexible and can be configured to meet a variety of needs.

LIST SERVERS

The list server is no more than the computer and associated software that manages a particular discussion list. Servers are frequently found at colleges and universities, where they can be used to manage many different lists. Commercial servers can also perform this function. Servers must be dedicated; i.e., constantly available, thus they generally cannot be used for other purposes. The expense of purchasing such dedicated systems and of installing phone lines, combined with the easy availability of public or commercial servers, usually discourage individuals from setting up their own list servers.

LIST TYPES

Announcement Lists

Members of announcement lists receive information posted by the list owner. Many email newsletters are distributed this way. For example, large publishers may offer email announcements of new publications. You might visit a publisher's Web site and type your email address and book interests into an online form to add yourself to the publisher's newsletter. Then they will notify you automatically when books of particular interest are published. Or perhaps you have visited an interesting site dedicated to Web site creation and design. Perhaps they publish a monthly email-based newsletter with marketing and design tips. If you subscribe to these services, you are subscribing to an announcement mailing list. You cannot respond to these announcements, nor can you make comments to be distributed to other list members. You will never know who else has subscribed or how many recipients there are.

Announcement lists serve a particular need. You can use them to obtain information from a particular source on a regular schedule. If you have an interest in Web-based marketing, but lack the time or inclination to routinely search for updated information on that field, an announcement list might just serve your purpose. Once found and subscribed to, they appear regularly in your "inbox" for your review or deletion.

Discussion Lists

Discussion lists allow people to *exchange* information. List members can reply to messages posted by other list members. In some cases, these replies are sent to the list server and then distributed automatically to all list members. In other cases, the list is configured so that replies are sent only to the person who sent the original message. How a list is configured to reply has a major impact on the type and amount of discussion. A list in which replies are circulated universally usually has "livelier" discussion. A list that permits only private responses ensures privacy, but usually has more limited, less dynamic discussions.

Tens of thousands of email discussion lists exist. List members share common interests with participants around the globe—a remarkable development in communications that especially benefits freelance indexers. There are a large number of discussion lists that may be of special interest to indexers. Some focus on indexing techniques and practices; some on education and professional development; and others on running a small business, marketing, computing or other skills.

The primary discussion list for indexers is *INDEX-L*. Serving approximately 1100 members, it is a rich and eclectic resource. Topics range from erudite debates on theoretical issues to discussions about general marketing approaches or how to determine whether indexing is the right profession for you. The interchange is generally lively, marked by abundant and diverse opinions. In short, it is a place to which indexers can turn for advice, answers, and encouragement.

Other lists include *TECHWR-L* and *TechComm* for technical communications; *WISP-L* (Women in Scholarly Publishing List); and *Copyediting-L*, which address specialized interests and information needs.

Because a discussion list exists does not mean that it will be successful or useful. For success, you need a receptive target audience. For instance, *INDEX-L* is aimed at indexers and other interested professionals. It reflects the participation of a broad spectrum of individuals with experience in many different areas. Other lists have a smaller target audience and, as a result, a more narrowly defined scope. Some of these specialized indexer discussion groups include *aliaINDEXERS* for Australian indexers and interested others; *WINDMAIL* for those involved in Web indexing; *Indexstudents* for those interested in indexer training, education and professional development; *INDEX-NW* for regional (Pacific Northwest U.S. and British Columbia) indexing issues. For information on these and other mailing lists, see the American Society of Indexers Web site page on discussion groups or check a mailing list search engine, such as Liszt. (See Resources at end of chapter for Web site addresses.) Despite the size of a list, there must be a need for it or it will fail to generate subscriptions or participation.

Digests

When you first subscribe to a list, you may be given optional ways of receiving messages. You may choose to receive individual messages as they are distributed by the list server or you may prefer to receive messages at specified intervals. If you choose the latter option, all messages will be listed in a single email message called a digest. Many lists compile a digest of each day's messages and send them out at the end of each day. However, servers may limit the number of messages that can be contained in a single digest, so if the discussion is active, several digests may be sent out during a single day.

Types of Email List Users

Despite the availability of the lists described above, there are still many possibilities for the creation of mailing lists that will serve large groups of indexers. Having said that, let's consider what segments of the indexing population can benefit by further list creation. How can existing lists be better used to advance the interests of individual indexers and the profession as a whole? What kinds of new lists are needed? Let's look at some broad categories of email list users.

Organizations

Organizations, including the American Society of Indexers, its chapters and special interest groups (SIGs), indexing groups, and other professional groups, can benefit tremendously from having a discussion list centered on the group's mission and philosophy. A good example is the recent establishment of *ASI-L* for discussion of topics specific to the American Society of Indexers. In the past, ASI members have used *INDEX-L* as a venue for discussing ASI-related issues, but non-members complained about having to filter out unwanted messages about internal ASI matters. Now *ASI-L* gives ASI members an opportunity to discuss ASI-related issues without involving non-members. *MSITalk* is another example. It gives members of the Massachusetts Society of Indexers a chance to discuss chapter-related business. For information on these and other mailing lists, see the American Society of Indexers Web site page on discussion groups.

Both the organization and members benefit from the creation of this type of list. Information can be disseminated to the membership (or at least to those who subscribe) quickly and efficiently. This can reduce postage costs. Also, members can provide feedback critical for avoiding misunderstandings and facilitating decision-making. A sense of community and commitment can be fostered. Further, responsible and timely communications improve the confidence of members in the organization's leaders.

Conversely, there are potential drawbacks. Not all of the membership is likely to subscribe, raising the possibility that too much attention will be paid to the concerns of a vocal minority. The organization's leaders must be careful to ensure that the discussion list is only one means of soliciting input from members. A skilled list moderator is needed to keep discussions focused and professional. As a result, email discussion lists may increase the time that the organization needs to spend on administrative functions.

Some of the specific ways an organization can use email lists include:

- As a resource for disseminating and soliciting information. Organizations can post requests for expertise and individuals with the required experience can step forward to help.

- As a sounding board. An email discussion list serves as an ideal place to "fly" ideas and trial balloons. Feedback can give shape and credence to the final product.

- As a means of maintaining contact with related organizations. Inter-organizational discussion lists can provide an easy forum for discussing ideas of common interest. For example, a new list might involve the governing boards (or designees) of the major international indexing organizations [the American Society of Indexers (ASI), the British Society of Indexers (SI), Indexing and Abstracting Society of Canada (IASC) and the Australian Society of Indexers (AusSI)].

- As a campaign tool. Candidates for office can make their positions known to the membership. The membership can have a chance to ask questions to determine the competency, skills, and energy of candidates. In most organizations, the membership does not have the opportunity to get to know their elected officials in any meaningful way.

- As a resource for brokering jobs. Organizations can post job openings and act as a clearinghouse for their membership. This would require having a system in place to solicit jobs for members.

- As a tool for planning and conducting meetings. Smaller organizations or components of large organizations can use discussion lists to help members "meet" via email, flexibly, and without requiring them to travel or be at their phones for conference calls. For instance, a chapter may set up a list to discuss upcoming chapter events. A special interest group (SIG) could hold an online forum to plan marketing or professional development events.

- As a networking tool. In all of its incarnations, a discussion list helps members get to know each other. Introductions are made, common interests are discovered, and bonds are formed. For freelancers, this can be as valuable as the professional and technical support such lists might offer.

Managers and Participants in Group Indexing Projects

Anyone who has managed a large project (database indexers, in-house indexing teams, freelancers working on shared projects) from start to finish knows that good communication is the key to success. An email discussion list is an ideal way to keep a team of individuals "on the same page." In some cases, project managers may want to broadcast information to team members using an announcement list. In other instances, discussion may be integral to developing the project.

Some specific uses of email lists in this context include:

- As a tool to disseminate information to team members. An announcement list is ideal when there is a lot of information with little need for discussion or feedback. Announcement lists can be used when decisions are final and the team is composed of informed professionals who know what to do. In a discussion list format, members can keep the team informed of their progress by posting periodic status reports.

- As a tool to develop policies and procedures. When the scope and direction of the project are evolving and input from team members is desirable, a discussion list can allow everyone involved to speak their minds and contribute to the development of the overall plan. Each member can give and receive feedback, discussions can develop rapidly and consensus can be reached quite easily. Advantages of discussion lists include low cost, the ability to provide visual examples, and scheduling convenience (participants contribute at times convenient for them).

- As a management tool. What happens when individuals become ill or when new team members are added? Supervisors can delegate new responsibilities or shift duties, using the list to keep team members up to date.

- As a quality control tool. Using email, team members can develop and share controlled vocabularies, acronym definitions, and stylistic requirements. Discussion lists allow individuals working on complicated projects to make sure they are following the same protocols and using the same terms and approaches. This is especially valuable for freelancers who may be working at sites distant from the project manager and other team members.

Individuals

Freelance indexers are sole proprietors in every sense of the word, defined by their individuality and self-reliance. Usually they do not work as part of a team. The Web and email allow indexers to work successfully in remote locations. Using abundant online resources and efficient email services, freelancers can conduct research, interact with clients, and provide finished indexes without leaving their homes, without suffering from this remoteness. By participating in email discussion lists, they create a virtual office environment that can provide technical information, business advice, and personal support.

For individual indexers, email discussion lists can be used for:

- Information. *INDEX-L*, to name just one list, is often besieged by requests for information. What are the sorting conventions for Vietnamese names? How do you handle glitches in indexing software? What rates should you charge for indexing periodicals? The questions are endless and the answers varied. Lists are a repository for experience and knowledge (a "collective wisdom" as both *INDEX-L* and *Copyediting-L* have been called).

- Finding jobs. There are lists specifically designed for posting jobs. For example, *LIBJOBS* is dedicated to promoting opportunities in the library science field. There are other, more subtle, ways to use discussion lists to land jobs. Most lists allow you to "lurk" without contributing, and you might consider monitoring some lists as a way of identifying job opportunities. The Publishers Marketing Association, for example, maintains a discussion list that deals with issues important to small publishers. By making intelligent contributions to such a list within the framework of posted rules (perhaps with a clear signature line that spells out your business), you may attract some clients.

- Professional development tool. If you would like to improve some of your indexing skills, you might try a list like *Indexstudents*. As a list geared toward indexer education and training, it offers short learning exercises online, and longer ones are often arranged among individual indexers. If indexing is a second or part-time career, you might want to maintain contact with the field you worked in previously. A mental health professional could continue to participate in psychology discussion lists; a chemist in a chemists' list. You can even use "hobby" lists to make your name and indexing skills known.

- Networking. As noted earlier, communication is a form of networking. Networking doesn't mean simply broadcasting your message; it often means volunteering time or knowledge. Those indexers on *INDEX-L* who are most respected (and most likely to receive referrals from other indexers) are those who make intelligent, frequent, and considerate contributions to the general discussion. Put your best foot forward.

- "Water cooler" chats. Finally, an essential benefit of a discussion list is for relaxed, informal conversation with professionals who share your interests. In some cases, professional lists, such as *INDEX-L*, frown on "off-topic" discussions (for instance, pets or homeschooling). Other lists, such as *Copyediting-L*, seem to relish mixing casual relaxed banter with more professional postings. If you want the opportunity to hang around the virtual water cooler, you may decide to create a splinter group of professional acquaintances who are similarly interested in establishing a place where you can engage in non-professional talk.

CREATING YOUR OWN EMAIL DISCUSSION LIST

Let's say that you decide to create your own discussion list, or you have been asked to create one as the manager of an indexing team. How do you go about it? You'll need to make some decisions about the type of list, the list server, and the subscribers. You'll need to publicize the list and manage any disputes. You may need to nurture it if discussion is slow. Here are some things to think about.

The first decision that you will need to make is where the list will be located physically. Where will the server be? How will you run it? What level of control do you want? These decisions depend on how comfortable you are with list technology.

Dedicated Servers and Software

Many universities operate a system of list servers on which they allow individuals or groups to place discussion lists. A list administrator watches the system log and other files, looks for errors, helps new owners set up lists (such as yours), and manages list archives. This type of server usually uses special list management software (Majordomo and Listserv are two popular types). You will need to follow whatever rules or policies are in effect for lists on that server. These usually encompass commercial content, advertising, and decency issues, among others.

The list owner is the person who manages the list on a daily basis. As list owner, you will need to learn how to set the various parameters of the list, how to establish subscription types, how to establish "Reply To" settings, provide digests, and other related items. In addition to many books and Web sites that provide information about running list management software, there are discussion lists for list managers to confer about the trials and tribulations of running a discussion list.

Commercial Mailing List Services

Several commercial mailing list services have cropped up over the last few years, including Onelist, Hotmail, Listbot and others. These services offer free list hosting services to list owners. In exchange, the hosts attach short advertisements at the end of each message. One advantage of a commercial service for list management is that little, if any, technical knowledge is required. These services are usually Web-based, meaning that you can go to a Web site and change list functions easily by selecting various options.

MANAGING AN EMAIL DISCUSSION LIST

List Parameters

Whom do you want to subscribe to your list? What type of information will be posted? How much participation do you want and how can you structure the list to promote discussion? Here are some things to think about when deciding on the list parameters.

- Do you want an announcement list or a discussion list? Do you want primarily to broadcast information to subscribers? Are you producing a newsletter with a regular publication schedule? Will you want or need feedback from list members?

- Will your list be moderated or unmoderated? A moderated discussion list follows one of two models. In the first type, all postings pass through the moderator (you or a designee) for approval before being passed on to the list server for distribution. Depending on the number of subscribers, this can be very time-consuming. In the second type, the moderator monitors the list discussion, intervening only when serious disputes or problems arise (such as subscribers not following the posted rules of the list regarding content or advertising, posting attachments to the list, or simply being rude). It is not clear to what extent the moderator (or the host) of a list can be held liable for the defamatory or biased remarks of subscribers. In an unmoderated list, no one watches to insure compliance with the list rules, and participants have free reign to post on nearly any subject, subject only to the guidance and feedback of other list members.

- Do you want open or closed subscriptions? The list manager can choose to approve subscriptions so that only certain individuals are included or excluded (e.g., allowing only ASI members in an ASI discussion group). A closed subscription list helps to keep the list focused on the original mission. Closed subscriptions are ideal for organizations, chapters, SIGs or other membership-based groups. An open subscription essentially means that anyone who finds the list can subscribe to it. Open membership usually leads to a broad, more diverse discussion.

Policies and Procedures

Once you have decided on a list, its focus, server location and list parameters, you'll need to develop a set of policies and procedures for individuals to follow when posting to the list. These can be simple or elaborate. You may start with a few simple rules, then add to them as issues arise. On lists dedicated to discussion of professional matters, a common policy concern is whether commercial messages or advertisements can be posted. Other areas requiring policy decisions include the length or frequency of messages, the subject matter of messages, the use of inclusive language (so as not to offend individuals or groups) in messages, "flaming" (sending disruptive attack messages) and "spamming" (sending multiple unsolicited advertisements to list members).

No matter what policies you decide on, enforcement is essential. If a discussion list's policies are routinely flouted, chaos ensues. List members will unsubscribe and the effort will fail. On professional lists, disruptive individuals are rare, and careful monitoring by the moderator usually takes care of any problems that arise. The policies should include consequences for breaking the rules the first time, the second time, and specify conditions under which a member can be removed from the list.

List Publicity

Once you have established your discussion list, you'll need to promote it in order to attract subscribers. Depending on your focus, you may have a built-in audience. A chapter list will naturally include the chapter members. You'll need to notify them of the list's existence, provide subscription information, and follow through by helping them subscribe. The same can be said for specialized and narrowly focused lists like those for special interest groups (SIGs) and team indexing projects.

A broad-based list, with a large and diverse potential membership, requires more extensive publicity. New lists should be registered with some of the online mailing list compilation guides (Liszt, for example). They should be promoted on existing mailing lists to which potential members might already have subscribed (respecting, of course, those lists' rules regarding commercial messages). You could create a Web site that includes information about the list, with a member area or FAQ (Frequently Asked Questions file). Professional organizations that might be interested in your list should be notified; you can help things along by providing an article about the site for them to add to their newsletter or Web site. Word-of-mouth is usually the most effective method of attracting subscribers, and a well-run list will generate such discussion and subsequent subscriptions.

Fostering Discussion

A successful list requires a lot of initial effort. You might need to generate discussion topics, foster a sense of community among the members, and encourage comment from those who are shy about participating. Commonly, lists are composed of 10% posters and 90% lurkers; the large number of lurkers should not be a cause for concern. If the content is interesting, the list is meeting the needs of both the posters and the lurkers (or they would unsubscribe). Success is measured in different ways for different lists. High volume is not always desirable. Ten or twenty messages a day may be too many for members to handle easily and may cause them to unsubscribe. It all depends on your group.

You may need to do most of the initial posting of messages until the membership reaches a self-sustaining level. Or you may need to respond privately to each person who posts, thanking them and encouraging them to continue participating. The "Reply-To" settings are of paramount importance when trying to foster discussion. If your list is configured to reply only to the individual sender, there may be considerable private discussion among list members, but not much group discussion. This may suit your needs and the needs of the list members. Many lists, however, are configured to send replies to the entire list. This promotes general public discussion; however, the "Reply-To-List" setting has the potential to distribute privately intended messages to the entire list, sometimes causing embarrassment to participants.

Mediation

People have opinions and like to express them freely. The nature of email makes it difficult, at times, to discern the true nature of a message. Tonal inflection and physical gestures are absent, resulting in misunderstandings and conflict. Humor often misses its mark and can quickly backfire, causing new problems. These are issues for you, as the moderator, to be aware of and to warn others about. Often no intervention is needed, but when it is, it's best to remain as neutral as possible. State the policies of the list, avoid mentioning individuals by name, and try to be fair.

Private messages to the individuals involved often help. You won't need the diplomacy skills of the Secretary of State, but you might want to cultivate some of them.

Privacy

Subscribers to your list may have some expectation of privacy (either regarding their messages or addresses). It is your job as list owner to explain the privacy policies of your list. If you use a commercial server, familiarize yourself with their privacy policies, post these to your list, and make sure they are known and understood. Archives of list messages are often kept by the server. Will these be made available to the general public or only to list members? So long as you make the policies clear, you have done your duty. Potential subscribers can then make informed decisions about whether or not to participate.

The most egregious error a mailing list owner can commit is to deceive list members about what will be done with the information they provide. In the case of commercial servers, a registration process is often involved. Potential subscribers are asked to provide required information, such as their email address, and optional information such as their real name, address, phone number, interests, and occupation. Be sure you and your list members know what will be done with any information. In most cases, it is used to compile demographic profiles (i.e., number of subscribers in a geographic area, number listing a specific occupation) used to set advertising rates, and no individual information is sold or distributed. Make sure you know the policies.

CONCLUSION

As you can see, there are many existing email lists available for you to explore. Despite this abundance, there are many reasons to create new lists. If, for example, as a member of an existing list you feel there is too much discussion focused on a specific topic, perhaps it means there is support for an entire list dedicated to that topic. If you belong to an organization or project team and feel it could be more productive with improved communication, then perhaps a discussion list would help.

Email lists are full of possibilities. The most successful and useful ones are clear in their scope, well supervised, and active. With a clear vision of the potentials and a firm understanding of the restrictions, you can do a lot to make sure your list fulfills its mission.

RESOURCES

American Society of Indexers Web site, particularly the page on discussion groups
http://www.asindexing.org/discgrps.htm.

Listbot, http://www.listbot.com/. Free mailing list management

Liszt, http://www.liszt.com/. Search for mailing list topics; free mailing list management

OneList, http://www.onelist.com.. Search for mailing list topics; free mailing list management

Glossary

absolute URL. An address that shows the entire path to a file, including domain name, path, and file name; e.g., "http://www.somesite.org/library/doc3.htm". Absolute URLs are used when referencing a page on another server. *See also* **relative URL; URL**.

Active Server Pages (ASP). A browser-independent server-based technology from Microsoft for building dynamic and interactive database-driven applications with HTML and scripting languages. Users can access data in a database, interact with page objects such as Active-X or Java components, or create other types of dynamic output. Typical applications include customized Web sites and complex database applications.

anchor. A marked location in an HTML document (e.g., a Web page) that a user can jump to from another location. Also known as a target.

announcement list. Email list that sends subscribers solicited announcements, newsletters, other types of information; subscribers may not post messages to other subscribers on the list.

applet. Small application written to accomplish a specific task, e.g., a calculator, clock, game, scrolling message, or interactive event. Usually written in Java programming language, this is also called a Java applet.

architecture. The structure of a Web site, database or other document with multiple components. Also known as information architecture, architecture includes structures and navigation systems that provide users with quick access to desired information.

authoring software. A software program that helps Web designers create HTML or multimedia documents, often in a WYSIWYG environment. The required codes are automatically generated by the authoring software.

attributes. Options for HTML tags that allow a Web site designer to further define the formatting desired. For instance, the link (<A></A>) tag has several attributes, including HREF and NAME. The HREF attribute allows you to define links to other Web pages or locations within the same page; the NAME attribute allows you to create anchors on the linked page.

browser. A software program that allows you to read hypertext documents on the Web, on an intranet, or on your own computer. Popular browsers include Netscape Navigator and Microsoft Internet Explorer.

button. A circular or rectangular image on a computer screen that a user can "click" to make a choice, activate a link, or cause something to happen.

CD-ROM (Compact Disk-Read Only Memory). A compact disk with read-only memory, capable of holding hundreds of megabytes of digital data.

CGI (Common Gateway Interface). A method of communicating with the server to cause something to be done. CGI scripts, usually written in Perl language, are commonly used with forms to send the information typed into the form to a designated recipient or otherwise process the information. Many ready-to-use CGI scripts can be downloaded free from the Web.

chunking. In embedded indexing, chunking is receiving portions of books in separate batches. In indexing, chunking is separating out ideas or pieces of information into manageable concepts to be indexed.

chunking out. In embedded indexing, eliminating previously included chapters after indexing has occurred.

classifying. In computer book indexing, creating long lists of subcomponents under a single main index heading, such as a specific type of menu or dialog box.

clip art. Small, usually copyright-free, artwork that can be reproduced electronically for use in word processing, desktop publishing, or on Web or intranet pages.

code. Programming or scripting instructions that direct computers to do what they do.

comment or comment line. Information included in computer code that identifies the purpose of the code or provides instructions to the programmer, but is ignored by the browser.

compiling. In embedded indexing, the automated process of generating an index from embedded indexing tags.

counter. A display, usually located at the bottom of a home page, that shows how many times the page has been visited.

desktop publishing (DTP). Using computers to create, design and produce books or other documents. Also known as electronic publishing.

DHTML (Dynamic HTML). The use of HTML, style sheets, and scripts (commonly JavaScript) that allow a Web page to change after it is loaded into the browser, in response to user input. For example, text can change color or size; graphics can move from one location to another.

digest. A group of email messages accumulated over a set period of time, sent to recipients in one file rather than individually.

distribution list. An email list where members exchange information, usually focused around specific topics.

divider line. Horizontal rule created with the <HR> tag, used to separate portions of a Web page. An <HR> tag has several attributes, allowing a choice of line width, height, alignment, and shading. HTML 4 suggest the use of Styles, rather than horizontal rules.

document chunking. *See* **chunking.**

domain name. Unique name identifying an Internet site; for example, "asindexing.com" or "usgs.gov". Domain names must be registered with InterNIC.

electronic publishing. *See* **desktop publishing**.

email (electronic mail). The sending and receiving of messages over the Internet.

embedded indexing. The process of inserting index entries in the form of tags placed into document files. Embedded index data can be edited electronically and compiled to create an index.

entry, index. *See* **index entry**.

FAQ (frequently asked questions). On Web sites or email groups: a list of answers to common questions about specific topics of interest to site users or group members.

flaming. Sending personal attack messages either via a mailing list or on an electronic message board.

floating text. In desktop publishing, text contained within an electronic document that can move as formatting changes.

frame. The division of a Web page to allow the display of more than one Web page at a time. Often used for site navigation or as a means of page organization.

full-text search. The process of searching through every word in a document, rather than, for example, searching <META> tags or using an index to find information.

freeware. Software that is distributed free-of-charge to users.

GUI (graphical user interface). A visual and usually mouse-activated system for entering computer commands, in contrast to a system in which commands are typed in manually. GUIs usually include icons, a cursor (mouse-activated), windows, and pull-down and pop-up menus. Both Macintosh and Windows use GUIs.

headword or head entry. A title word or term placed at the beginning of an article in an encyclopedia.

Help index. Index to an online Help program or program component.

Help topic. In online Help, the keyword that leads users to discussions of specific topics of interest.

hit. A visit to a Web site.

home page. (1) The opening page of a Web site. This is the primary jump-off point to other locations within the Web site and usually has the file name index.htm or index.html. (2) The page that the browser is set to display to when it is opened by the user. This might be a news site, a search site, the user's own site, or some other site that the user visits frequently.

horizontal rule. *See* **divider line**.

HTML (HyperText Markup Language). A markup language used to create hypertext documents for the Web, using a set of codes (tags), in ASCII files that any computer can read. Tags are used to create links and add graphics, sound, video, text, and formatting to Web and intranet pages.

HTML editor. *See* **authoring software**.

HTTP (HyperText Transfer Protocol). The basis for the transfer of HTML-formatted documents over the Internet.

hyperlink. An HTML-based construct that allows a user (a) to move ("jump") from one location within a hypertext document or Web page to another document or Web location, or (b) to perform certain Web-based actions, such as sending electronic mail. *See also* **HTML**; **hypertext**; **link**; **URL**.

hypertext. A method of presenting information electronically that allows users to move from one point to another in a non-sequential way.

index entry. A "line" in an index that may include text, page numbers, cross references, or hyperlinks. An index entry typically contains a main header, subheadings, page ranges or links, and cross-references. *See also* **link**; **locator/locator text**.

index tag. In embedded indexing, the code inserted into electronic document files to identify main entries, subentries, and locators.

information architecture. *See* **architecture**.

inter-document link. A link that leads you from one point in a document to another point in a second document.

Internet. The world-wide system of linked computer networks that allows the widespread exchange of information. The Internet is used for email, file transfers, access to the World Wide Web, electronic commerce, and other communication and exchange purposes.

intra-document link. A link that leads you from one point in a document to another point in the same document.

intranet. A closed system of linked computer networks that is usually restricted to communications within a single organization or group.

ISP (Internet service provider). A company that provides users with access to the Internet.

Java. A programming language that is used to create small programs (applets) that can be transferred over the Internet and provide special effects such as animations, games, and calculators.

JavaScript. A scripting language designed to add interactivity to Web-based documents.

JPEG (Joint Photographic Experts Group). A file format (.JPG or .JPEG) used to compress graphic document for faster transmission and easier storage. Often used for photographs and other complex art.

keyword. A word that has special meaning within a specific context. In online indexes, keywords are often used as links. In <META> tags, keywords are terms that describe the Web page and may be used by search engines to retrieve the pages.

link. In HTML documents, an element of a document (a word or graphic) that provides a connection to another point in either the same document or another document. *See also* **hyperlink**; **inter-document link**; **intra-document link**.

list administrator. The individual who oversees email list system logs and helps manage list archives.

list owner. The individual responsible for day-to-day email list operations.

listserver (listserv). A program (e.g., Majordomo) that automatically distributes email messages to a selected group of recipients.

live file. In embedded indexing, the electronic file that is currently being edited, formatted, or indexed.

locator/locator text. An identifier that tells the user where the information is within a document. In back-of-the-book indexes, locators are usually page numbers or page ranges. In online (Web) indexes, however, the heading or subheading may also serve as the locator text, becoming a unit of linked text. Alternatively, a symbol or number may be used as the locator in an online index.

lurker. A member of an email discussion group who receives messages but does not participate in the discussion.

manual. A text designed to teach readers how to use specific hardware and software. *See also* **tutorial**.

markup language. A set of rules for adding meaning to text, often through the use of tags defining how a document is to be formatted. *See also* **HTML**; **SMGL**; **XML**.

menu. In Windows-based systems, a list of choices or options, the user can select, often with submenus, or further breakdowns of options available.

meta data. Files that contain information about the data, rather than the data itself. Used for managing and navigating around databases.

<META> tag. In HTML, <META> tags are used by the Web site developer to provide hidden information about a Web page, its contents, author, and related information to search engines and to cause certain actions, such as redirection to another Web page.

MPEG (Motion Picture Experts Group). A formatting and compression standard for audio and video files.

multimedia. A general term for an application that combines text, sound, graphics, video, and interactivity.

multiple indexes. More than one index for a document. Multiple indexes may be broken down by subject matter or type of material. The most frequent example is the use of both an author index and a subject index.

NAME attribute. An attribute used in several HTML tags to provide additional information. In the <A> tag (anchor tag), the NAME attribute is used to create a name for the anchor; in the <META> tag, the NAME attribute is used to specify the type of <META> tag used.

navigation system. Document components that let users move around a document or from one document to another. Scrollbars, hyperlinks, arrows, menus, and buttons may all be parts of the navigation system.

network. A group of inter-connected computers.

Online Help. Electronically available Help information that can be accessed within a program.

page proofs. In regular publishing, typeset sheets showing pagination; used to create back-of-the-book indexes.

product-oriented indexing. In computer books or Online Help, product-oriented indexes are lists of terms relating to commands and chapter headings that depend on the user's having an understanding of the product and its components, rather than terms relating to what the user wants to do with the product. *See also* **task-oriented indexing**.

programming language. A language used to write the instructions that get computers to do what they do. Examples include Visual Basic, Cobol, Lisp, Java.

relative URL. Also called a relative address. A form of the URL that shows the relationship of one Web page in a site to another, rather than its absolute (complete) address. For example, if two Web pages are in the same directory, a link from one page to another can be simply the name of the page file: "doc3.htm", rather than the complete, or absolute URL: "http://www.somesite.com/library/doc3.htm". A system of forward slashes and periods is used in relative references to Web pages in directories that are higher or lower in the directory tree than the referencing page.

search engine. A Web-based program designed to search a single site or the Internet. Users usually enter specific terms and the engine returns a hyperlinked list of sites that contain those terms. Different search engines work differently; they will return different lists of sites for the same terms. Popular search engines include Yahoo, AltaVista, Dogpile, Excite, HotBot, and Webcrawler.

See also **reference.** In indexes, a reference used to point the reader/user to related topics.

See **reference.** In indexes, a reference used to redirect users to other locations where that topic is addressed. *See* references are used for vocabulary control, to avoid duplication, and to save space.

server. Part of the client-server relationship; a server provides services to clients. On the Web, a server is a computer where a Web site is located or software program that responds to requests submitted by the client (the Web browser).

setting the page break/breaking the page. In desktop publishing, the process of formalizing and locking the locations where page breaks occur.

SGML (Standard Generalized Markup Language). A standardized set of codes used to add formatting to ASCII documents. SGML allows the cross-platform transfer of electronic documents and is the precursor of HTML and other markup languages. *See also* **markup language**.

shareware. Software programs that are usually distributed free-of-charge. However, users are often asked or required to pay the author a fee if they intend to use the program on a continuing basis.

signature. In book publishing, separately bound 8-page sections that make up a book. The number of signatures in a book, or the number of pages left over in a signature at the end of the text pages, may limit index size.

SIG (Special Interest Group). A group whose members share specific interests, e.g. science and medicine, history, gardening, or Web indexing.

slipping. The fluid movement of schedules, usually applied to the delivery dates for projects or project segments.

spamming. Sending multiple unsolicited advertisements via email.

spider. A type of search engine that finds and indexes Web pages, and includes them in a database from which search results are selected.

stand-alone index. The index that appears at the end of paper documents. In contrast to embedded indexes, they are usually created with dedicated indexing programs and kept in files separate from the document itself.

tag. Hidden code in text files that is used for creating embedded indexes, adding formatting, creating links, and other purposes. *See also* **embedded indexing**; **HTML**; **<META> tag**.

task-oriented indexing. In computer books or Online Help, task-oriented indexes describe procedures from the user's point of view, adding terms that help to describe the procedure: technical and non-technical synonyms, common vocabulary from the workplace, or widely used terms from other products. *See also* **product-oriented indexes**.

tutorial. A step-by-step teaching method, especially for computer-related topics. Tutorials can be teacher-led, self-directed, text-based, computer-based, or Web-based.

URL (Uniform Resource Locator). The address of a Web site that identifies the location of the site and allows users to access that site with the use of a browser. *See also* **absolute URL**; **relative URL**.

user interface. The mechanisms that allow users to interact with their computers. The most commonly recognized user interface is a Windows screen. *See also* **GUI (graphical user interface)**.

VBScript. Microsoft's scripting language for adding interactivity to Web pages, using a subset of the Microsoft Visual Basic language. VBScript is often used with Active Server Pages (ASP).

Web browser. Software designed to view Web pages. Netscape Navigator and Microsoft Internet Explorer are the most common Web browsers, but there are numerous others.

Web indexing. (1) A list of links to external Web sites, annotated or not, usually on a specific topic or related topics, organized alphabetically, by subtopic, or by some other system. This is also referred to as "indexing the Internet" or "indexing the Web." (2) A hypertext index to the contents of a specific Web site. This can be similar to a back-of-the-book or journal index, or it can take on a new form, more like a navigation system than a traditional index.

Web page. A single, usually HTML-based, document that is viewed by a Web browser.

Web site. A linked set of Web pages.

Web-based documentation. Help or other technical assistance available on the Internet.

Web-site content. The information, data, articles, images, applications, and audio/visual files that the visitor sees, hears, or experiences when she or he visits a Web site. Content is separate from style, which is the way that information is formatted and presented to the visitor.

white space. An important element of good Web site design, white space is the blank area on the screen that divides up and provides structure for the text and images, helping make the page more readable and aesthetically pleasing.

World Wide Web (or Web, or WWW). The HTTP-based network of individual Web sites accessible through the Internet.

web. A private HTTP-based system, usually part of an intranet.

WYSIWYG (what you see is what you get) program. A program for Web site development, HTML authoring, wordprocessing, or desktop publishing that displays on a page as it will appear on the Web site or on the printed page, rather than the codes that create the formatting.

XML (eXtensible Markup Language). A language for describing a document's structure and meaning, allowing Web developers to define their own markup tags. XML is especially useful for managing the style and format of a Web site.

Index

by Janet Perlman

Chronologically based subindexes, 53
Chunking, 14, 134
CINDEX®, in online indexing, 63, 65
Circular cross-references, in Web indexes, 49, 52
Classifying, 22, 28, 46, 134
Clip art, 134
Closed subscription list, discussion lists, 129
Code
    defined, 134
    indexing techniques for, 20-21
Comment line
    defined, 134
    indexing of, 21
Common Gateway Interface (CGI), 134
Compiling, 6, 9, 134
Composer (software), 63, 103
Computer software
    embedded indexing, 3, 6, 7, 10, 15-16
    freeware, 135
    graphics programs, 103
    Help system authoring software, 91, 95, 97
    HTML authoring, 63-64, 74, 102-03, 108-09
    indexing archives of, 34-35
    <META> tag generation, 31, 74, 76
    multimedia programs, 103
    online Help indexing, 91, 95, 97
    shareware, 139
    thesauri, 30
    Web authoring software, 102-03
    Web indexing, 41
    Web page design, 102-03, 111
Computer-related documents, indexing, 13-23
    acronyms, 22-23
    author contact, 14
    embedded indexing, 3-11, 15-16
    indexing techniques for, 16-20, 22-23
    manuals, 16, 18
    online Help indexing, 89-97
    payment rates, 11, 13
    programming texts, 20-22
    scheduling, 15
    space limitations, 14
    work process, 14
Computers
    embedded indexing, 7-8, 10, 15-16
    Web page design, 103-04
Constructs, indexing of, 21

CONTENT attribute, 73
Copyediting-L (discussion list), 123, 127
Counters, 33, 134
Cousins, Garry, 82-83
Creating Killer Web Sites (Web site), 112
Cross-references
    CD-ROM indexes, 80
    circular, 49, 52
    function of, 61, 138
    online Help, 91
    Web indexes, 48-49
    Windows-based online Help indexes, 95

D

Dan's Web Tips (Web site), 76
<DD> tags, 64
Deadlines, computer-related documents, 15
Definition lists, 64
Description tags, 71-73
Design
    indexers as part of design team, 30, 84-85
    Web indexes, 48, 50-54
    Web sites for indexers, 109-10
Desktop publishing (DTP)
    defined, 4, 134
    embedded indexing and, 4-6
    software for, 3, 6-7, 10
DHTML (Dynamic HTML), 134
Dialog boxes, indexing techniques for, 19-20, 22
Digest mode, 123, 134
Dimitry Kirsanov's Top Ten Design Tips (Web site), 112
Discussion lists
    announcement lists, 122, 133
    closed subscription list, 129
    creating, 127-28
    defined, 121
    digest mode, 123
    group indexing projects and, 125-26
    hosting services, 128
    indexers' use of, 126-27
    managing, 128-31
    moderated, 128
    open subscription list, 129
    organizations' use of, 124
    privacy issues, 131

Other Books on Indexing from Information Today, Inc.

The Indexer's Guide to the Internet, 2nd Edition
Lori Lathrop

The Indexer's Guide to the Internet, 2nd Edition, is a must-read for indexing professionals interested in learning about Internet tools and information resources. In this thoroughly updated, expanded edition of her 1994 book, former ASI president Lori Lathrop points readers to useful sites for indexers, while providing numerous informative how-to's, including tips on selecting equipment and service providers, locating other indexers and professionals online, deciphering Internet jargon, designing Web sites, and using Internet search tools. Also included are a helpful glossary and bibliography.

Softbound • ISBN 1-57387-078-1
ASI Members $25 • Non-Members $31.25

Indexing Specialties: Medicine
Edited by L. Pilar Wyman

This in-depth look at the indexing specialty field of medicine is the latest in the popular series from ASI and Information Today, Inc. With contributions from over a dozen noted medical indexers, the book features 13 chapters in four parts: "Medical Indexers" includes an interview with two veteran book indexers and a biography of a database indexer; "Medical Indexes" includes examination of award-winning medical indexes and medical index reviews; "Medical Indexing" gets into the heart of the matter and provides detailed discussion of indexing medical specialties, with chapters on indexing food and nutrition, nursing, and general medicine, and three chapters on database indexing; and "Resources" lists guides to medical reference tools and Internet-based resources.

Softbound • ISBN 1-57387-082-X
ASI Members $28.00 • Non-Members $35.00

Directory of Indexing and Abstracting Courses and Seminars
Edited by Maryann Corbett
No matter what you want to learn about abstracting or indexing, this guide will help you find out where to learn it. Library professionals, online information designers, abstractor and indexer freelancers, and publishers' staffs can all find courses that suit their needs in the Directory. Included are courses from public, private, and proprietary institutions in the U.S. and Canada.
Softbound • ISBN 1-57387-056-0
ASI Members $12 • Non-Members $18

A Glossary
Hans H. Wellisch
This book includes terms used in writings on abstracting, indexing, classification, and thesaurus construction, as well as terms for the most common types of documents and their parts.
Softbound • ISBN 0-936547-35-9
ASI Members $10 • Non-Members $16

Marketing Your Indexing Services, 2nd Edition
Edited by Anne Leach
This is a collection of articles from ASI's Key Words, with additional chapters by Anne Leach. It includes strategies for beginning indexers and new business owners, as well as established professionals. An excellent addition to any freelancer's library.
Softbound • ISBN 1-57387-054-4
ASI Members $15 • Non-Members $20

Indexing Specialties: History
Edited by Margie Towery
This compilation of articles focuses on the indexing of history textbooks, art history, medieval and Renaissance history, Latin American history, and gender and sexual orientation language issues. The authors' intelligent advice and discussions will assist both new and experienced indexers who work in the field of history and related disciplines.
Softbound • ISBN 1-57387-055-2
ASI Members $12 • Non-Members $18